Relationships Matter

CHANEL N. SCOTT

13TH & JOAN

For permission requests, write to the publisher, addressed "Attention: Permissions Coordinator," 205 N. Michigan Avenue, Suite #810, Chicago, IL 60601. 13th & Joan books may be purchased for educational, business or sales promotional use. For information, please email the Sales Department at sales@13thandjoan.com.

Printed in the U. S. A.

First Printing, July 2023.

Library of Congress Cataloging-in-Publication Data has been applied for.

ISBN: 978-1-953156-95-2

DEDICATION

Thank you, God, for loving me through every trial, misstep, heartbreak, and loss, and for teaching me that my most important relationship is the one I have with you.

Love,
Chanel

TABLE OF CONTENTS

FOREWORD

RELATIONSHIPS MATTER COULD very well change the landscape in ways similar to the "Venus and Mars" epitaph by helping men and women take a more honest look at the way we interact with one another.

Scott's willingness to reveal intimate scars and wounded hopes is laudable. Every lesson you learn from love allows you to move closer to your destiny and personal fulfillment in that area.

Scott's commitment to transformation and self-reflection makes her own love story even more of a divine possibility and she has graciously invited us along on the journey.

The fact that Scott has not yet found her own "happily ever after" makes her story even more powerful. So many struggle with patience in the process. Scott gives us a real time glimpse into the soul of singlehood and how to handle your own NOT YET.

When audacity and courage engage, while truth and transparency embrace—you get a book like Relationships Matter.

This book speaks to the core of one of the most coveted desires of the heart... to be partnered in a loving and healthy romantic relationship. These pages unearth true intimacy in a raw and relatable way.

In her own quest for healing and growth, Scott has created a narrative that brings priority and purpose to the relationship conversation again. It reconnects us to days gone by when two people came together for a reason greater than themselves. And it was common place for a man to be asked, "What are your intentions in dating my daughter?"

Relationship intentions are being reimagined through these pages and redefined with the live platform of CheMinistry.

Scott has successfully created a space where relationships are not just a hot topic...but a place where RELATIONSHIPS actually MATTER.

Nevaina Rhodes
Drama Therapy Specialist and
Intimacy Coordinator for
BET's Kingdom Business
Games People Play and
The Ms. Pat Show

IT'S A MATTER OF RELATIONSHIP

THERE IS NO such thing as a perfect relationship. Every relationship has both healthy and unhealthy characteristics. However, what makes the connection strong is when both people in the relationship have a willingness to put in the challenging work necessary through candid conversations to recognize unhealthy behaviors that could be detrimental to the relationship as a whole. Oftentimes, people talk more about avoiding toxic people and less about overcoming the toxic behaviors that contribute to the tension in the relationship. More so than not, we know what our toxic behaviors are, but we don't necessarily know how to disengage their triggers.

In this book, we lay out the blueprint to communicating our feelings in a more productive way that not only nurtures but deepens the romantic connection shared by those who are intentional about growing their romantic relationship.

MAKING IT ALL MAKE SENSE

A ND NOW, IT all makes perfect sense. My life as a single woman has been negatively impacted by an unusual amount of rejection. I have suffered through and overcome depression as my life ended up in a stalemate some years ago. Rejection and subsequent depression became a norm for me. In every relationship, another woman was chosen over me or so I thought. In past relationships, I was angry, aggressive, and in some of the more extreme situations that involved cheating and blatant disrespect, I was volatile. The social rejection I endured in those failed relationships led to anger, anxiety, depression, sadness, and even jealousy. I used to think that romantic relationships were a competition where only the most attractive or those with more to offer were partnered up first while the rest of us were resigned to a life of loneliness.

I was born in Henderson, North Carolina. I am an only child to my parents. My mother told my father that the only way she would have sex with him was if he married her. My parents married when my mother was 18 years old, and my father was 23. My mother described my father as a "cheater" when they were together. He was a semi-pro baseball player, and she said women had a natural "affinity" toward him. My mother tells the story of how she was miserable during her pregnancy because he cheated the whole time. His cheating forced her to make a tough decision, so 11 days after I was born, my mother left my father and moved us to her hometown of Newark, New Jersey. After being separated for nearly a year, my mother moved back to North Carolina to try to rekindle the flame with my father, but by that time he was expecting another child by my mother's best friend which gave me a younger sister in the process. My mother wanted to make the relationship work and went back to my dad three or four times, but resented him for what he'd done. She couldn't bear the sight of him and didn't even allow him to touch her. I remember one time she told me that my sister's mother was in her house and when she got there, my father wouldn't open the door. She busted out the windows of the house and my father had her arrested. My grandmother who lived in New Jersey at the time came to pick me up. She took me back with her while my mom stayed in North Carolina until her court date and to resolve the charges.

Once my grandmother and I returned to New Jersey, I was surrounded by family who absolutely loved me. My grandparents took me to church every Sunday and I loved to sing in the choir. My mother eventually came back to New Jersey and life seemed to be normal until she began dating a man who was physically abusive toward us. He would fight my mother in front of me and give her a black eye. I was 4 years old at the time and remember him making me get on my knees, with my hands behind my back, then beating me. I used to suck my thumb a lot and would get a blister on it from time to time, but in the midst of him hitting me with a belt, it would burst which was equally painful. When my mother saw all of this she jumped on him which then became a fight between the two of them. These events were part of a cycle where they would break up and get back together. Eventually, my mother became pregnant and gave birth to my younger sister.

The only decent memory that I have of this man is being taught how to do multiplication. I hated when my mother left me with him, and I am sure that my frustration was expressed in some manner; most likely vocally. I had a very smart mouth (still do today), and must have said something, even as a 4-year-old child, that triggered him because he smacked me very hard across my face. I would see cocaine around his nose while he was at our house. He was definitely on a destructive path due to the heavy drug use and being physically abusive as well. He was in and out of jail, which was on par with his lifestyle, but I don't think anybody, including myself, could've predicted what would happen next. My mother told me that she had prayed for deliverance from this man. She wanted God to remove him from her life. A prayer that happened on a Friday was unexpectantly, and most of all tragically, manifested on the following Tuesday. On this day he was taken out of my mother's life and everyone else's too. When all of this occurred, I was visiting my father in North Carolina. While there, I received a phone call from my mother telling me that he died from a drug overdose. Later on, she found out that he suffered from visceral congestion but had been doing drugs at the time of his death. I was 8 years old, and my sister was two at the time. My mother was now a single parent with two daughters at the age of 25. Looking back, I don't know how she survived. My mother struggled to take care of us, and as times got hard, unwise choices were made on our behalf despite the good intentions. She began to sell drugs and move kilos of cocaine to make money which was a risky lifestyle to say the least. That career path was short lived because eventually, someone made a kidnapping threat against us, so at 10 years old, my parents decided that I would live with my father in North Carolina and my younger sister went to live with her paternal grandmother.

My mother and father always did a great job at co-parenting. I had already been traveling as an unaccompanied minor between New Jersey and North Carolina on an airplane since the age of five.

Once my father remarried, I was finally able to live in a two-parent household. My stepmother was an amazing woman who treated me as if I was her own daughter. As a child, I thought my father and stepmother had the perfect marriage, but sometimes children are not as keen on what is unhealthy and toxic in a relationship. I have two brothers; one younger and another that was my age. I said "was my age" to indicate past tense because tragically he passed away only two months after me moving there. My stepbrother was killed in a house fire along with his uncle and cousin. It was hard to find anything to be thankful for that Thanksgiving break. While another cousin survived, my stepbrother was gone. When I reflect back on the incident, I don't remember there being a lot of conversation around it. Sure, we all grieved, but I don't remember my stepmother being able to mourn like a mother should after the loss of a child. Many years later, I talked to her about it, and she said my father never allowed her to grieve the loss of her son. He wanted all of the attention so grieving would have been a distraction from his point of view. She backed the assertion by vividly recalling a visit with her family shortly after my step-brother's death. Instead of spending time with loved ones, he wanted her to leave the family and come home with him.

A couple of years after we lost my stepbrother, my dad found himself entangled in a "situationship" with the same woman that he'd impregnated during his first marriage to my mother (her ex-best friend). He got her pregnant...again and this time she gave birth to a son. I stayed with them a lot while growing up. My father would drop me off at their house and she was always good to me. During the Christmas holidays, she would buy two of everything for my sister and I. She and her girlfriend would always argue about it which I didn't understand back then. "Why would her friend have an issue with her buying me gifts?" I thought to myself. What I didn't understand back then is understood now that I am a grown woman. I realize that she should've set healthier boundaries between her and my father. I remember calling her on the phone one day after having my own "entanglement" with a professional baseball player who was also married to another woman. She warned me to get out of the relationship. She said that she'd spent a good portion of her life loving a man who didn't love her back. During that same conversation I asked her, "why were you so good to me?" to which she answered, "I loved your father." Thinking back on all the many lessons my father taught me, the one that sticks out the most was the act of "forgiveness." He always told me to work through conflict that may exist with my friends and never go to bed on my wrath. Now I realize why forgiveness was so important to him; he needed a lot of it.

Oftentimes, my mother would come to North Carolina to visit me. During those visits my father would let her drive his car despite being married to my stepmother. While unaware when it happened, my stepmother would always find out about it which made her suspicious of my mother because my father would do it behind her back. They managed to work through her hesitancies regarding my mother and to be honest, she had moved on. My father and stepmother eventually divorced because she learned that he'd cheated on her. I love my father, but he destroyed his relationships with negative patterns of behavior that would eventually ruin two marriages. These same unhealthy and toxic behaviors that I witnessed growing up had a profound effect on my own relationships.

My first experience with social rejection came at the age of eight. Although I was too young to be thinking about boys, I still remember the sting of that rejection. My feelings were hurt, and I felt unworthy even at such young age. I've suffered a tremendous amount of rejection in my life and to make matters worse, it stems from my own family. As a teenager, my aunt once told me that I was "awkward." Her words often held a lot of weight with me, so I was inclined to believe her. Besides, how many 15-year-old girls stand 6'1"? The boys liked shorter girls, so I always felt like the odd person out which meant that sex was not happening for me at that point. Many of the other girls my age were already sexually active by the time we got to high school. Some of my friends already had an experience or two by the tender age of twelve! I wasn't doing anything at that age but did have a "near" sex experience during my sophomore year in high school.

There are conflicting stories about how it happened but, here's my story in my own words. We were on an ROTC field trip to Washington D.C. when I and a friend of mine who also played basketball conspired to have sex on that field trip. The stars aligned and we were ready or so we thought. We got caught red-handed and with our pants at our feet! We didn't get a chance to do anything so I took it as a sign to wait which is exactly what I did. It wasn't meant to be at that moment in time, so I had to be patient. It took a little bit more time, but two years later, at the age of 17, I had my first sexual encounter with this guy who was also on the basketball team. We seemed to have a real connection. We took our school pictures together amongst other things. Everything seemed to be going great until it wasn't. I had to call a foul on the play when I found out from his own mouth that he had sex with a girl from his church. We took more than a timeout after he told me that because this was clearly a flagrant foul 2 which in basketball, is an automatic ejection. So, instead of charging it to the game, he was disqualified and ejected from my love life.

Later that summer, while visiting my family in New Jersey, I had my first "real" relationship. I met this guy the previous summer, but he was four years older than me. He lived up the street from my grandmother, and we'd sit on the porch with our friends and just pass the time talking about whatever. When I returned the following summer, we decided to explore a romantic relationship. Since I was only visiting, I was grossly unaware of his other relationships. On my last visit to New Jersey before leaving for college, I found out that he was expecting a baby with another woman. The pain, anxiety, and jealousy were all too overwhelming for me to manage. I was old enough for sex, but not the emotional pain and drama this relationship subjected me to. My man was having a baby with another woman...That's the kind of betrayal I don't wish on any woman!

We tried to make it work, but the pain lingered and the drama of it all made it a nightmare! On its own, the situation was bad but adding lies and manipulation to the mix created a recipe for failure! He lied to me about the true nature of their relationship but once I went to her house to confront him, things came to a head! Actually, we came to blows! She told me that they were in a full-fledged relationship but at seven months pregnant, she broke it off and put him out.

He came outside to confront me and then it happened...I punched him, and it was on! The "Thrilla in the Hallway" went down, right outside her front door! I had given him much more than my body; he was the first to have my heart but the emotional pain took forever to subside. My reaction that day was part of a pattern of reactionary toxicity in my life. See, I would only respond this way when triggered. I was known to throw fits of rage because of my unbridled emotion and these behaviors often surfaced in romantic relationships with each blowup increasing in intensity.

While writing this, I sought an ample definition for what I felt in those explosive moments. As it turns out, it's ineffable and incalculable. In other words, I was reacting to feelings that lacked articulation or quantification from my own understanding. I was in pain watching the man that I'd given my heart, mind, and body to choose another woman over me. I would love to tell you that my love life improved, but this scenario was on replay in most if not all of my relationships. That scene in the hallway was on repeat as well. I was always ready to fight a man because of how rejection made me feel. Do you know that feeling? Rejection made me feel unlovable, unwanted, and plain ole ugly! It took considerable time to learn it, but I finally realized that rejection is not a reflection of personal failures and flaws, but that of a relationship mismatch. While I know this now, it was hard not to personalize each instance of rejection as it was happening.

With all the drama and heartbreak behind me, I set my sights on UNC-Charlotte, and my life changed overnight. Rejection was a thing of the past from my vantage point. I had a new lease on life in a new city and a new campus! I had the attention of the more popular guys on campus; the basketball players! I was tall and a "girly" girl and they loved having someone on their level, so to speak. While they enjoyed my presence, it was overwhelming for me in a much different sense. The attention was all new to me because I'd never experienced that level of interest from boys before.

For starters, these weren't boys...these were men, and they knew exactly what they wanted! Still, I was shy and didn't know how to "talk" to guys. I was socially inept and didn't know how to respond when the most popular guy on campus tried to strike up a conversation with me. He was persistent and I was petrified! We didn't talk much because I was always too nervous to respond when he tried talking to me. Finally, he got one of his teammates to introduce us and it worked. After all the avoidance and awkwardness, I was in an actual conversation with the most popular guy on campus. We spoke on the phone regularly and he would always invite me to his apartment while we were on the phone. I consistently declined but one day, curiosity got the best of me. On that particular day, I ended up at his apartment and one thing led to another. I reluctantly had sex with him but felt that it was needed to get his attention. In my mind, once we had sex, he was my man, but I quickly found out that life doesn't work that way. I had been in his apartment and even his bed, but what we weren't in was a relationship. With this revelation, I was again faced with the same feelings of the previous summer!

Imagine the earth-shattering heartbreak that rocked me to my core when finding out that I wasn't his type. He liked white girls and being fair-skinned was no substitute for his real desire. I internalized this rejection deeply because there was nothing that could be done. He liked what he liked. I'm not white and couldn't buy him stuff like those girls did. Through growth and maturity, I discovered that people aren't always what they seem. He had several siblings and had grown up extremely poor. The silly women entangled in his web bought him clothes and spent their money on him. The only person he loved was Ms. "Basketball" and I think he was smitten by their money!

We don't often talk about it, but many of the men in our lives have hurt us because they didn't love themselves. The heartbreak we've experienced was the result of two people trying to love themselves through someone else! After my heartbreak with him, I set out on a path to "do better" than him but this unwitting competition only did more to damage my already low self-esteem. I was without purpose and from my warped perspective, I saw their rejection of me as a reflection of who I was as a person. I eventually learned the truth about him and so many others afterwards. There's always a back story to the life they present. They use smoke and mirrors to deflect from the truth of their life that we know nothing about; or at least they try to. Their inner turmoil has everything to do with them and not us. Many times, they project hurt into the relationship and onto people who love them to deflect attention away from their painful truth which only serves to protect their emotional fragility.

In my pursuit of validation and self-worth, I turned my attention to professional athletes. The first was a man I dated who went from college to the NBA. He was drafted at #4 and boy, did my life change after that. Before you start romanticizing life as a girlfriend of a top-five NBA draft pick, let me tell you that it was horrible! For starters, we were in a long-distance relationship after he was drafted. He wanted me to leave school and move with him to Minneapolis where he would be playing, but I was still in college and had no plans of leaving school. It didn't take long, but after about a month or so, I got a call unexpectedly. The girl on the other end of the call told me that my man, the draft pick, was cheating on me. She knew of me and had seen my pictures and read my letters. That wasn't even the worst part though! She was upset that he was also cheating on her!

You read that right! He got another woman pregnant, and not long after in the same year, she would also be adding a bouncing baby to his tribe! This is not the part of the book where I tell you that we broke up. I went from girlfriend #1 to side chick because unfortunately, I just didn't know how to let him go. In my quest to not only fit in, but also hold on to a man who was no longer mine, I toyed with the idea of sharing him with the multiple other women who were having his babies. Yes, that actually bounced around in my mind for a little while, even though I knew it would have been an unwise choice. Instead, I resorted to more impulsively aggressive behaviors with each new revelation of infidelity. I finally conceded that continuing on in this situation was not ideal for my life and definitely detrimental to my already low self-esteem so the decision was made to move on.

Back in Charlotte, I turned my attention to another baller who lived in Atlanta but played for the Los Angeles Lakers. He and I met while he was on the road with his team in Charlotte. We talked regularly but didn't see each other much because of the distance and I was still a student in college. The summer after we met, he was traded to the Atlanta Hawks. In hindsight, I recognize that this relationship wasn't really a relationship at all! Why, you ask? Every time I came to visit him there was always a woman in the background. If it wasn't that, I was being treated like an "extra" while in town visiting. I remember on one occasion, he let his friend ride in the front seat and forced me to ride in the back seat when we were supposed to be spending time together. On a separate occasion, I was left behind because he simply didn't want me there. There was a time that I really wanted to spend New Year's Eve with him, but he told me not to come. In the past I might have stayed put but this time was different. I drove down to see him and pretty much ignored what he said. Once I arrived at his house, a woman that I didn't know greeted me at the door and let me in. She said he wasn't home but told me I could come inside of the house and wait for him to come home. Once he arrived, I was blown off again. He told me that he would be with his friends for NYE and set me up in a nearby hotel.

The next day, I returned to his house. The front door was unlocked so I let myself in. I didn't know that he wasn't home, but I wasn't alone in the house either. I went looking for him when another unknown woman greeted me...in his bedroom! I thought that was strange, but stranger than fiction, he told me that I had to leave once he finally came home!

He put his hand on my shoulder to escort me out and I hit him square in the face! I should add that I have grown a lot since that time in my life, and I, in no way shape or form condone partner violence of any kind. To his credit, he never raised a hand in retaliation, but I fought him all the way to our cars outside. We both left but that wasn't the last we would see of each other. We kept in touch over the years but eventually we would end up in a more volatile situation. It was Memorial Day weekend, he came to meet me in Miami, Florida and stayed in a room I'd booked for him. I was a flight attendant at the time and I'd flown there with some of my girlfriends on a weekend getaway. One night, I called his room, but he wasn't himself. He didn't sound right, and I didn't know if I was more concerned or suspicious. Something seemed off and he abruptly ended the call. At that point, I had heard enough and was convinced that I needed to get over there to see for myself what my suspicions had already led me to believe.

My friend and I went to the room, and I instantly regretted it. From the hallway, we heard him and another woman in the room having sex! The devastation was unreal, and I was so broken, again. To think that nothing I'd done could keep a man was enough to send me spiraling into an existential crisis. I had done all I could to accommodate these men. I compromised my values and placed self-respect on the back burner in a feeble attempt to earn just a piece of their love for me. I gave away all the irreplaceable things that were mine due to a blinding lack of boundaries. Time, energy, and love were all wasted on these men with virtually nothing left for me.

Though I was left holding the bag in my chronically unsuccessful romantic relationships, I was killing the game and had secured the bag a few times over, professionally. By the age of 30, I owned a home and drove a nice luxury car. As much as I tried, success on the outside was no match for the void that persisted on the inside. It seemed that with each height I gained in my professional life, there was a new debasing low experienced in my love life. I was empty inside and looking for love in all the wrong places. I did things that I shouldn't have and let men misuse my body thinking it made me more desirable, but it only led to more rejection.

I was tired of the dysfunction and cleaned up my act, or so I thought. I wasn't fooling anyone at all! I went back to church, but had yet to face the dysfunctional behavioral patterns that spun the cycle of self-destruction. I thought church was a safe space and wanted to take a break but didn't realize how broken I was. I settled into regular church membership but didn't confront the issues that kept me broken, I wasn't healing, but merely self-medicating through church services. Once I realized that feeling good could happen without altering anything, I was alright but unbeknownst to me, a rude awakening was in my near future! In the place where I felt the safest, I experienced the worst heartbreak of all.

Worse than infidelity, worse than my boyfriend having a baby with another woman, and worse than any other pain I'd experienced before, the pain of heartbreak coupled with church hurt isn't pain, it was trauma! Life as I knew it came to an excruciating halt as I watched the man for whom I believed God had told me would be my husband marry someone else. I'd been rejected before but none of those outside relationships materialized in marriage during those times. This was different though! I wasn't even safe from rejection in the house of God! Making matters worse, it was a man of God doing the rejecting, this time! Life came crashing down on me and in the midst of it all, I lost everything. I'm sure that you're curious as to how all this happened and there's no need to keep you in suspense. Let me tell you about my season of "imminent death."

IMMINENT DEATH

YOUR DECISIONS CAN inevitably determine your destiny. We can make some great decisions that lead us down a path toward success while others can be regrettable and lead to our demise. Let me tell you about a time where my insatiable desire for a husband and my erroneous decisions literally ruined my life. I made a decision that would eventually lead me down a path of loss, grief and despair, not to mention the rejection that brought on the excruciating pain of a heartbreak *and* severe depression that led me to be stuck in a life's mess. I not only lost things but I literally lost Chanel, I lost my identity. I was resentful, unforgiving, bitter along with a wide range of emotions that gripped me with destructive passion. I called this season "imminent death" because my life was being destroyed by my decisions, so physical death would have been a surprise to no one.

I was caught up in a world of demonic manipulation and plain old foolishness. Have you ever heard the phrase, "you're breaking your own heart?" That was me! I watched the man that I thought God told me was my husband marry another woman. Before you go all black sitcom love story on me, know that this was different. He was single and, on the market, so it made sense to me. Now before you judge me, I want you to understand that single men and women have a right to try and get to know each other. He was actually a widower at the time and had begun a new normal which included entertaining women like me. A relationship just wasn't meant to be, but I stood on what I believed, and it blinded me. Because I was blind to reality, I missed the warning signs of personal turmoil headed my way. Before this saga ended, I was homeless, unemployed, friendless, and alienated from the church family that I loved so much. I thought they loved me, but unfortunately the world saw a version of myself that was insufferably ill. My car was repossessed, and I even filed bankruptcy. My whole life was in a tailspin, and it all came crashing down. And why?

"He is your husband." I wholeheartedly believed that those were God's words to me about a man that I had hoped would be my life's partner. My insatiable desire for a husband drove me headlong into a hellish situation with only myself to blame. I wish I could tell you that he played me like all the other men. I wish I could tell you that he is not the man he portrays standing behind the pulpit of his mega church. I wish it were him, but it was all me! Well, part of it was him. It all began at a church revival in Charlotte, NC as I watched and listened to his dexterity with the Word of God. His vocabulary was so pristine, piercing, and poignant, with each sentence. His command of the English language reminded you of his Princeton pedigree. It was a life-changing experience being under the auspices of this expert orator as he stood at the lectern but once the service ended, I found myself under the influence of his effortless charm while at his product table. He was handsome, witty, and did I say single? Though he wasn't exactly my type, something about him piqued my interest.

He was a published author and that added to the intrigue. I decided to solve some of the mystery about him by purchasing his book. He signed it for me, and I decided to visit his church with a friend the following week. I emailed his assistant to let him know that we would be traveling from Charlotte to Nashville, TN to visit his church. After the church service, my friend and I bumped into his assistant on our way to the front of the church to greet the pastor. He spoke to us and, my eyes just lit up with excitement because he remembered me. I spoke to the pastor briefly to say hello and that was the gist of it. After we left the church, we sat in the parking lot in awe and discouraged at the same time but that's when my mobile phone rang. It was the pastor! We spoke briefly and planned to meet later that day. I was so shocked by the experience of talking to this man that it alerted all my senses in such an unassuming way. He invited my friend and I to his home and we graciously accepted. We watched movies and played games before he showed us his musical talent on the piano. Time had flown by and it started getting late, and since we had driven from Charlotte, he invited us to stay overnight. We took him up on the offer and we continued playing pool and black jack throughout the night. We left the next morning and what looked to be a defining moment was solidified after the visit. I was greeted with "good morning" texts and a few phone calls, but that was short-lived. After a few weeks, the calls grew increasingly infrequent and finally stopped. However, I continued watching his church service every Sunday and the word of God was so piercing that I knew God assigned this pastor to speak directly to me. I'd longed for a transformation in my life, and could finally feel it happening! As with all transformations, there comes a season of transition. I was transforming and transitioning but not in ways conducive to my overall well-being. All manner of relationships were affected; work, church, and home, but I couldn't interpret what was happening. After losing my job in Charlotte, I made a crucial mistake, the linchpin that brought my world crashing down. About 5 months after meeting this man, I made the decision to move to the city where he pastored. This crucial decision was made all on my own. He didn't invite me, there were no subtle hints to uproot myself; there was nothing. Actually, there was no real romantic connection, just a concocted reality that proved detrimental. I left everything and moved to the city that I'd only visited once for a man I hardly knew.

I'm sure you've heard stories like this before. You've seen it play out on film or even in love songs (if that's what you'd call them), but the fact that the object of my affection was a pastor adds layer upon layer of complexity to my story. You see, I wasn't the only person vying for his attention. I wasn't the only woman seeking to get to know him. He had members to care for, a staff to lead, a personal life on the mend and a global ministry to oversee. Once I arrived in Nashville, the first thing I did was go to church. It was the first of many Sundays under the same roof and official leadership of the man that I believed would one day be my husband. I hadn't traveled to Music City to simply be drowned out by mega ministry, another woman, or to simply slip through the cracks of broken communication. I kept the lines of communication open at first, and got a reply, but it was only to let me know about his busy schedule and he was seeing someone! *Record scratch* Excuse me, what? That's the exact moment that I should have stopped and prayed or simply packed up for Charlotte, but I believed God would work things out in His own time. And I'd just moved there the day before. I could have saved myself money, heartache and did I mention money? Over the course of the conversation, he asked about my work situation. Since I had no other plan than to be with him, there was nothing that I could tell him in that moment. I had nothing lined up at all. He told me that as a member of his church our interaction would have to be different. I got the message, but I didn't take the hint until I called again about two months later. This call was vastly different. He told me that his life was in a different season and that his circle was fairly small. This was the message: He was no longer interested! This was quite embarrassing, but I feel that sharing this will help you avoid these same pitfalls. By this point in the story, I've been given two chances to drop the idea that this pastor would be my husband. "God" told me, and that settled it. I am resilient, but the resilience that should have sent me back to Charlotte kept me in Music City drowning in dissonance.

There weren't many mixed messages, and I don't think we got our signs crossed. I was committed to my own downfall. I doubled down on this message that he would be my husband by manipulating the Word to fit my own agenda. I was unaware that something deeper was happening to me. Out of a sincere desire to know God better, I intensified my pursuit to bring this word to pass. I decided that I needed to dress the part of "First Lady," so I created a public persona that precipitated the first stage of failure for me. As destructive as this was, it seemed to somehow be working... against me! After about 10 months of being in Nashville, he introduced the church to an "extraordinary woman of great significance" but, to whom? I had thrust myself so deeply into despair that I could no longer decipher that the output was a manipulation of the Word. I was in total darkness because I extinguished the true light of the word and substituted it with my own desires. As it turns out, the woman that he mentioned before was of great significance to him and just a month later, he stood before the congregation to announce their engagement. If this were a story in the Bible, that would most certainly be the moment when the Lord would make himself clear! Three times it was communicated to move on and possibly even back to Charlotte, but I ignored it each time. Come to think of it, I wasn't blind, I was deaf! Hear me out though, he had only met her two months before they were engaged. They married a few short months after their engagement and while they rode the high of newly wedded bliss, I experienced the debasement and depression and a death blow to my self-esteem. I was spiraling to new depths and was suffering through an existential crisis. I didn't know my purpose and had no identity. I didn't even know that woman, but lost my own joy trying to compare myself to her. With no joy left in my soul, I turned my frustration and anger on the Lord and blamed Him for the situation. I was so far from Him despite me being in the church and continuing to serve there as well.

As I do self-reflection even while writing this chapter, I know why I stayed. I wanted to show God that I was committed to Him and that my being in Nashville, actively involved in church had nothing to do with the pastor but more so about my relationship with Him and because I was blind, I thought I could serve my way out of this situation. I still struggled privately about whether or not this man was my husband, but more importantly, I turned my attention to God. I needed a SAVIOR. I was faithful to my post on the marketing team and remained in position waiting for something to happen but it never did. I endured in Nashville much longer than I should have and it cost me my mental health. I was tormented daily. I suffered from clinical depression and I didn't even know it at the time. What I thought was persistence was more like subsistence. There was nothing keeping me in Nashville but prideful ignorance. I didn't know that I was headed in the wrong direction because well, things hadn't quite come to a head, yet. After losing my home, I briefly lived in a dorm with a former mentee of mine at Tennessee

State University. I would travel by bus daily to serve at church. My car had been repossessed at this point. Some good did come out of this traumatic experience as I tapped into purpose in the midst of this hellish situation. I was making an impact on the marketing team and oversaw a project that generated over $30,000 in a span of six months. The team was so excited about the project that the pastor's assistant brought the news to him. He sang my praises, unaware of the familiarity we had with each other. As you can imagine by now, this news wasn't well-received, and the pastor brought my motives into question. I was doing the job that was given to me and my only desire was to be a blessing to the church. Sure, I was struggling badly at this time but there was no intention on my part to highlight anything about me. All of the controversy unfortunately led to a meeting with the director of HR which focused solely on my past interaction with the pastor. I was initially told that all volunteers leading major projects would be in the meeting because of the church's sudden, exponential growth. To make matters worse, I was confronted with the belief that the pastor was my husband.

The pastor acknowledged that he knew me, but didn't disclose to anyone that I and my friend had been in his home. He represented it as if we barely knew each other and not as if we were singles in communication with each other at some point. He painted a picture of me as a delusional person but never revealed the whole truth about us. In hindsight, I can confess to some strong delusion, but he could have at least told them that his number was in my phone! By this time, I had known him for three years. I secretly battled this misnomer about him being my husband, but the unthinkable happened when he involved the church in our mess. I was eventually told that the church leadership was unsure about the motives behind my service to the church. By this time, I was hanging on by a thread while battling depression, homelessness, the loss of my car, and demonic manipulation. Threatened with the loss of what little stability remained, I gave up and went home though still not quite away from it all. I struggled to let that part of my life go because I continued to keep tabs on things in Nashville. The death knell was the birth of his daughter which consequently fell on my 38th birthday and is a day that I will never forget. For me, that day signifies my lowest point in that saga. Not only was he not my husband, but he also moved on, married another woman and their child shares a birthday with me. Of all the ways for God to exact his punishment on me for manipulating the Word and believing a lie, I still thought this was excessive. How much could one woman take? There I was, a 38-year-old woman sharing bunk beds with her nephew at her sister's house with no positive outlook on the future in the forecast. When I got the Twitter notification on my phone and read that tweet, I went numb. My mind overflowed with painful memories. You know, the pain hurts worse when it's self-inflicted. With meager strength and mental fortitude, I decided, "it's my birthday, I'm going to celebrate today!" I picked myself up but on the way into the shower, the House of Cards had officially collapsed. I showered but in total darkness. The pain was too immense to fathom. It all hit me like a ton of bricks so all I could do was scream! The silent scream that began barking orders and telling me that this man was my husband was finally audible! It took many years and many more screams, but I was finally able to work through my private struggle. This was a compounded struggle; major depression was brought on by an erroneous belief in repetitive malicious manipulations of scripture. The root of it all? An intense desire for marriage which led me down one of the darkest paths of my life.

I'm sharing my story with you because so many of us need an outlet of expression in regard to our relationships. Talking about relationships in church seems so taboo and so many Christians seem content to watch the demise of their relationships as they suffer in silence. The church is even meaner to singles desirous of a relationship. You are rebuked if you even dare speak on your desire for a relationship or marriage. How did we get to this point? Shouldn't the church be the entity fostering the healthiest marriages and relationships? Instead, I was ridiculed or labeled "thirsty" or impatient by those who could have guided me into healthy and godly romantic perspectives. And where is the safe space for honesty and transparency? Where do people go to decompress and lay bare the emotional toll and spiritual challenge of abstinence, celibacy and simply finding "the one?" People have wised up and are tired of what I call "broken advice" as the standard. Epithets like "love yourself more," "learn how to be by yourself," and the ever popular "focus on yourself" do much more harm than good. They mean well but do absolutely nothing for people in pursuit of healthy romantic relationships with another person! If I learned nothing else going through this ordeal, I learned that God alone has the power to change your circumstances. I also thank God for protecting me while I endured the self-inflicted damage of believing that lie. I could have lost even more than I did but because of his grace, I can tell you my story with no lingering shame or sense of defeat. I'm also sharing it with you as a cautionary tale. The Bible says that with temptation, God provides a way of escape (1 Corinthians 10:13). I didn't escape, I was forced out because I ignored every opportunity to check in with God or simply double check my motives. I should have never gone to Nashville, but I did and stayed four years too long. Some of you reading this are in what you consider healthy, functional relationships but you too are blinded and deafened by your own desires. You're overstaying in a relationship that doesn't serve your best interest, while envisioning a future that will never materialize. You can't or choose not to see the rejection in your partner's words and actions. I implore you to keep God at the center of your relationship! If you are not currently involved but are seeking a relationship, just know that God should be the nucleus of your pursuits. He knows what's best for you and as I had to learn, he hears and sees what you can't or otherwise refuse to.

Today I reside in Atlanta, Georgia and God has given me a second chance at life and love. I think back on this season of life and shudder to think about what would have happened if that pastor labeled me as a stalker or some derogatory term. In all my time in Nashville, I can't recall a single conversation where he told me explicitly that our friendship was all that he desired. Maybe he thought I would get a clue, who knows. Maybe he prayed and asked God to remove me. Maybe he's a pacifist and doesn't really like confrontation, hence the subtle clues. In my case and so many others, the truth was implied but unspoken. Many times, we withhold our truth for fear of what another person's truth may be. When it is necessary to speak up, we should feel the safety to do so without retaliation even when the truth revealed is unfavorable. This led me to the creation of CheMinistry, a relationship platform. I sought to create a space where men and women could communicate openly about issues in romantic relationships. Of course, it helps when celebrities you see in movies and on television can join the conversation, so at each event, I'm joined by celebrity panelists. Together, we converse about a relationship topic and share life experiences to help the audience through their experiences with the topic. Most importantly, CheMinistry puts men and women in the same space to share their varying perspectives on a topic. We don't always agree but I make sure that we are all heard! Since the inception of CheMinistry, I have noticed the evolution of relational conversation. Couples communicate openly and are no longer afraid to talk about the issues plaguing their relationship. The best outcome of each episode is couples' willingness to face their issues together.

It's not surprising to me that men and women are diametrically opposed on certain issues and may never totally agree on everything, but the fact that we can at least talk about them is a victory unto itself. You can imagine the brows raised and side-eyes that I still get when telling this story. This is proof positive that its impact goes further than I can imagine. If my focus was on the faces of disgust, I would miss the silent cries whispering, "help me!" I'm here to help you, and CheMinistry is where relationships go to change for the better. I'm driven by an unforgettable trial and testimony and most importantly an unyielding, unselfish hope for amazing romantic relationships everywhere.

I wish that I could've went back home of my own volition, but there was nowhere else I could go after losing it all. I packed up and went home to live with my parents. Somewhere in the boxes were the answers to my life's questions. For the first time ever, I was unpacking the baggage of my past. Emotional trauma as a child, growing up in a broken home, consistent rejection, and overall feelings of unworthiness had to be unpacked. Why did I feel that way? Why did I accept such low standards in the men that I chose? I had to use the clues contained in the boxes, while reflecting on what I'd lost. The combination of the two would ultimately answer the question of, "how did I get here?"

For once, there was no one to blame, it was all my fault and I had to do the hard work of putting the pieces of my life back together. In 2015, I moved to Atlanta, Georgia in pursuit of a fresh start. I had been celibate for eight years (for me that means I hadn't dated anyone) so I made strides to get back out on the dating scene. You know, I wanted to show the world the new Chanel. "**Chanel 2.0**," if you will. What I learned in my time of reflection is that relationships were like kryptonite to me. In my professional life, I was super but the quickest way for it to all come crashing down was for me to be in a relationship.

I had already asked myself many hard questions, so it was time for one last step. As a successful, single woman who has never married nor has children, I want you to avoid the same pitfalls that plagued my younger years so, I created CheMinistry, a relationship platform, now a series regular on Fox Soul. The tv show aims to help bridge the gap between purpose-driven men and women who desire to progressively move their love life to the next level. We foster this understanding through candid and transparent conversations.

Because so many people struggle in the area of relationships, my goal for this book is to leave on record, lessons that teach you how to absolutely love yourself first, handle rejection gracefully and how to have healthy communication, boundaries, mutual respect, and support for one another. The CheMinistry effect accomplishes these tenets in a more productive way that not only nurtures but deepens the romantic connections between men and women. When men and women become intentional about growing in their relationship together, the possibilities are limitless!

YOU NEED THIS, NOT THAT!

NOW ALL I need is a husband! What more could Nashville Chanel possibly want? I had a great job, luxury car and nice house. The only thing left on my list was a husband. Like the rich young ruler in the Bible, I could hardly imagine that I lacked anything at all. A loving husband was all that was left off of my list and why wouldn't that be possible? To even ask God for anything besides that would have been rhetorical at best. Have you ever felt completed except for one thing? That was me until I discovered that the one thing I lacked was purpose and not a husband. God was intent on me finding that instead of love and what ensued was a war of the worlds and wills and the battlefield was Music City, USA.

This point in my life happened because God gave me the answer to a question I never asked. I wasn't intentionally ignoring God. In fact, I thought my pursuit of a husband was drawing me closer to God. As It turned out, I was only drawing myself further away from His plan for my life as I forced myself closer to the man I thought would be my husband.

That man wasn't my husband, and I never should have been confused about whether he was or not. Thinking back on the time we visited his home; I distinctly remember him telling me "this is not a defining moment." Of course, it wasn't, we were still getting to know each other, and I trusted that more definitive moments would come later, though they never materialized. As you've already read, moments of sheer kindness and generosity were conflated to mean more, which they shouldn't have. But, in the process of all I endured in that season, I discovered that God was providing me with the realization of purpose and not a husband.

I wanted to be married back then and still desire a fulfilling marriage, now. I do still believe that I will one day marry the man God has for me but let me tell you about this journey of purpose I'm on, now!

Had I never endured that season, I'm sure that I would have never created CheMinistry. I'm confident that no other set of circumstances or series of events would have prepared me to receive the healing and clarity this season provided me. There were more lessons to learn after I created CheMinistry, but this season was a landmark for me. This marker says, *never go back!*" and I carry these lessons with me every day and in each episode of CheMinistry.

As I told you earlier, I was successful, young, and ruling in my industry when I lost myself. The very thing I thought I lacked was the last thing God wanted me to have. Have you ever reached the point in your life where it seems that God is blocking all your prayers and refusing to grant your heart's desires? You know, sometimes you begin to think that something really is wrong with you! There has to be, otherwise, why would God suddenly ignore your requests? I later discovered that nothing was wrong with Chanel, but everything was wrong with what I desired and especially the way I chose to go about pursuing it!

I thought I knew God. I thought I had grown to the point that I knew what He wanted for me and that He would at least be willing to engage my requests of Him. "You made man, I'm sure you've got one of those for me. I'm ready for him now, please!" That's what the immaturity of that season sounded like. That prayer never works! If you're praying anything similar to that prayer, you're praying amiss with wrong motives or like me, praying it in the wrong season. What God wanted to give me was purpose and not a husband. Actually, He was showing me purpose and how to use what He was showing me in that season. I wasn't interested because I had a timetable that I was working with and learning about anything besides love and marriage was not on my radar!

This is the truest instance of God knowing our hearts. He knew why I was asking what I asked of Him, back then. He also knew how I would manage that man if we dated or even got married. Nashville Chanel was not ready to be that man's wife! At that time, I felt like I was ready to welcome love into my life. I was ready to be loved by a good godly man and I was ready to do all the things he would have needed me to do.

This experience was a hard "no" for me to process. It was an emphatic response from God because He made every attempt I made to win that man embarrassingly unsuccessful. Literally everything I tried either backfired or just had me out there looking crazy. I'm a very balanced person and I've grown to handle rejection with grace. I was unprepared to handle God rejecting my request, though. The harder I tried, the worse I failed. Nothing worked and all of the tenacity I poured into the pursuit of what I thought would be mine, the harder each defeat was to handle.

My soul was injured by the time I left Nashville. Imagine trying to move a brick wall, that's what my time in Nashville felt like. I was an emotional wreck and couldn't process how I'd lost everything just trying to add the one thing I felt my life lacked. Trying to move the unmovable will of God crushed me and He crushed me to show me purpose. In the midst of the breaking and ultimate crushing, I also learned that on the other side of that indestructible wall of God's will was His loving hand. Yep, He loved my bruised and battered soul back to health. He helped me see that His protection that manifested in the form of rejection kept me from imminent self-destruction.

It didn't feel like it at the time, but God's love for me made it all eventually make sense. I didn't have to look on the bright side to find the lesson, here. All I had to do was extract my will and desires from my time in Nashville to understand why God blocked every attempt at what I thought I wanted. He positioned me to learn what I needed for what He wanted me to have. It was only then that I gained an appreciation for Him blocking everything that wasn't for me. You will never be the right person for the wrong person, and you could never provide anything of value to anyone who has nothing for you! Why am I telling you this?

Many times, we ruin being around the right people and in the right places by trying to get from them or out of them what they aren't meant to be. That man was there to provide leadership and a spiritual covering and not companionship. This misappropriation almost ruined my relationship with God and him as a faith leader and gospel teacher. We were never meant to be lovers and never even came close to it because he was mature enough to communicate this and reinforce it. I then found my place as a student of his teaching and employed his wisdom in the building of CheMinistry.

By the time I left Music City, I had everything I needed to birth CheMinistry and flourish as we have to this point. This proves that all things really do work together, even when there's an ugly part to it. I think all of us have an ugly season to our lives. Some of our ugly seasons are self-inflicted while others are inflicted on us at the hands of others. Though it came with tremendous pain, this revelation was music to my ears! Did I have to go through everything I experienced to birth CheMinistry? No, not really! Much of it was because I was so stubborn, but the lessons learned actually strengthened my resolve. Looking back on Nashville, I learned that you will always get what God wants you to have. Many times, we look at our lives as if we didn't get what we wanted, but who says that's a bad thing?

Proverbs 19:21 says that we make plans but it's ultimately God's plan that will work out in the end. So just know that things will work out God's way whether we like it, understand, or even contribute to it! Remember, I wanted a husband, but God knew that I had nothing to offer him. I was a career woman living my best life, but what would that man be getting if he made me his wife back then? Would he even be interested in Nashville Chanel? You have to be honest with yourself when you sit in misery about what didn't happen.

Believe it or not, there are some people and things we would despise had we known the full truth about them when we desired them. I no longer question that season in Nashville because I clearly see that as a season of unleashing purpose in my life. I shared this portion of my life story as both a cautionary tale and encouragement to single people in pursuit of love.

Sometimes, the hardest thing to do is be happy as a single person. We all want love and a loving companion. Some of us have made a habit of settling for whomever enters our orbit and we never achieve the love we desire, though we have constant companionship. You deserve better than that! The Apostle Paul conceded that our need for companionship and intimacy often preclude us from seeking God on the level he did. He said that he wished that many could be like him, but he ultimately understood that it's not possible for most. I don't think I'm called to be a eunuch for the gospel like Paul but if that's you, you have my respect. I think I at least deserve a real shot at love, and I hope this time the Lord agrees with me. In this season of singleness though, I'm pursuing purpose and purpose alone has my full attention. Now, if you see me out and about with somebody's son, just know that it's with God's approval!

I've lived through the season when I didn't trust God saying, "*this, not that!*" But I can say that His plan for me is much bigger than I could have ever imagined for myself. His plan is greater than the pain I experienced in Nashville, and I have a voice now! I'm helping people who have experienced the pain I've experienced and I'm able to do it as a whole, healed woman. I'm not bitter and I'm growing in my faith and through my personal experiences. If you were to ask me, I'd tell you that I don't think that I had to lose to win, but I can testify to you that when your plans are in direct competition with God's, you will lose every time!

Singleness is not a curse, it's the status necessary to bring God's will to pass in my life and I like living this life, now. I'm single, successful and steadily reaching toward God's plan for my future! I'm secure in who I am, what I'm called to do and when the time comes, exactly who I'm called to!

IS IT LOVE OR LUST?

ANOTHER INSTANCE OF choosing the other thing when considering relationships is deciphering the difference between love and lust, which can be quite confusing. You call it love, but what do they call it? Clarity and confusion cannot coexist! Being in love with someone that is merely lusting after you will ultimately hurt you in the end. The revelation that you're only being tolerated for their sexual pleasure is a tough pill to swallow especially when you have emotionally invested into the relationship. You love all of them while they just love your body. You want to give them your world and, they're taking whatever you're giving! This is common and so is the heartbreak that this type of relationship causes. The Merriam Webster dictionary defines love as, "a feeling of strong or constant affection for a person. Attraction based on sexual desire; affection and tenderness felt by lovers." On the other hand, lust is defined as, "a strong feeling of sexual desire, and intense longing or craving. A strong desire for something." Now let's get something straight, some of us are lusting after love. You read that right! The intense longing and strong desire for love and to be loved has lowered our standards and has made us susceptible to committed relationships with people we know don't genuinely care for us. You remember my story in Nashville; I lusted after love, and it sent me into delusional behavior that no woman in her right mind could explain. I made something out of nothing and conflated innocent gestures to mean more than he ever intended. Women get so excited because of calls, spending time together, texting and having his attention, but are wary of the trap awaiting them. The excitement is blinding, and we become blissfully unaware that he has lost interest, things have cooled down and communication grinds to a halt. If you've chosen to make things physical, you can understand that sex is communication also. This is why we're confused! Sex is telling us that he's interested, but his actions or inaction is saying that he's not. Let's be honest, many times we haven't heard anything after things get sexual because the act keeps speaking and that's the only communication we hear! Unfortunately, sex isn't communicating desire for you as a person as much as it's saying, "I desire someone to have sex with!" If we tell the truth, we've had sexual chemistry and experiences with people that we should never have ever been physically, spiritually, or emotionally connected to. This reality makes it clear that we spent time serving the interest of sex and not our soul! With sex out of the picture or no longer an option, you're sure to discover the biggest void in your relationship is actually friendship. Many sexual relationships have thrived without a real connection, but I'm sure you desire and are unmistakably certain that you deserve better! Romantic relationships deserve better. They warrant the mutual input of nurturing from both partners but when lust contends with love, nurturing of love is impossible.

> *"This is why I think it's important to build a friendship*
> *before we fall into that oh, 'I think he likes me' trap."*
> CHANEL N. SCOTT

If anything besides mutual attraction and interest is the foundation of your relationship, expect it to fail. Before giving your body to another, make sure that you want to give them your heart and mind as well. Have you ever stopped to think about some of the people you don't like but had sex with? Maybe the realization came later installed during the progression of the relationship. It seems too easy to skip over like to lust. We don't spend ample time getting to know a person and ultimately pay dearly once feelings get involved because of sex. If overall feelings are not aligned we're forced to deal with heartbreak. Save yourself the trouble and force the issue of getting to know a person as a whole before agreeing to any sexual contact. Lust will never be a suitable replacement for all the joy and happiness that true love will bring, so equip your relationship pursuit with what it needs to maintain intentional clarity and emotional integrity. Relationships go through many phases. One minute you like each other and the next minute, not so much. Each relationship experiences rough patches, but what will keep it moving when threatened with stagnation? Shared goals will do this and that's why it's important for you to get to know one another! Has the relationship progressed to the point that you have shared goals and purpose? If you can't get the purpose piece right, the relational peace will greatly suffer. You must first define your collective "why." Why are you two together? Then, define what you seek to do together and lastly, clarify how you intend to do it. That's the relational piece.

You can already tell that communication is a major factor to the success of any relationship. It's not enough to articulate desires and plans, you must also be articulate enough to express how it gets done and develop communicative practices that reinforce them, recognize success, and course correct when needed. If you are going to have a successful relationship or marriage, you're going to have to communicate. Communication is much more than talking; it's listening and also understanding. As the relationship progresses, you must also learn how each of you communicate love. Remember when a woman would ask her man if he loved her, and he would call out bills being paid or maybe point to her hair, nails, and wardrobe? That man communicated love by spending money. However, most women don't receive deep emotional love as gifts. This impasse in communication was a direct result of tangible versus intangible expressions of love. Neither of them was wrong, but they failed to comprehend each other's communication of love.

We also know about the physical communication of lust disguised as love. There may be miscommunications, misunderstandings and even misdeeds done, but it's all made right by some good loving! Well, that's the thought but unfortunately not the correct answer. Lust distracts both people and never allows an earnest pursuit of a romantic relationship. Married couples aren't exempt from this phenomenon either. Lust is a strong desire and though it manifests in sexual acts most commonly, lust for riches, social status or very simply having your own way at any cost. Lust endangers any relationship that it's a part of.

Lust induces a toleration where exploration should be. Many times, you find yourself hitting a wall when trying to learn your partner while they force the issue of their desire on you. Unless forced to, I never discovered what authentic friendship as the root of relationships was, and this was my downfall. I regularly skipped steps in the "getting to know you" process. I went right to the "I like you. Do you like me?" phase to the detriment of every relationship. These relationships were baseless and empty because I knew nothing about the men I dated. Well, I knew that they liked me enough to have sex with me, but almost every relationship suffered a similar fate. Because we hadn't taken the time to build a friendship while pursuing romance, we were unaware of our commonalities and mutual interests. We were even grossly unaware of commonalities in the way we handled and mishandled conflict. There was no purpose in our being together so as time wore on, the relationship fizzled out. It took time, but I had to learn the skill of becoming friends with the man I had a romantic interest in. I always wanted friendship, but it wasn't long before I wanted more than that. I wanted it more because I didn't possess the skill of truly getting to know a person. I didn't really know myself nor did the person I was presenting to be loved and that was the most difficult hurdle to overcome. Because physical attraction was there, I thought everything would develop as easily, but I was wrong. You must become intentional about learning a person and the relationship you're pursuing or risk losing it to relational immaturity. Another factor hindering the exploitive process is fear. Our fear of what may be revealed when we ask questions keeps us only acutely aware of the person, we desire a relationship with. Truth is, in many instances, something that we can't handle. We can't handle the truth about past sex partners, family history, education, job status, salary, religion, children, or incompatibility so we simply don't ask! We resign ourselves to knowing as much as we can assume by watching their patterns and investigating what they allow us to see. If this is OK with you, are you sure that you're not the one lusting after something? As I mentioned before, a strong desire for a relationship or companionship will cause you to abandon sensibilities, overlook red flags and conflate even the most menial expenditure of effort.

Real love meets your partner's needs and not only what you desire them to have. Does your partner need to audibly hear that you love them? Do they need your love reinforced by how you take their feelings into consideration? Lust will bankrupt relationships by constantly withdrawing love expressed by sex and never replenishing the love tank because they make no investment into the relationship beyond what they can "cash out" via sex or other lustful desires. Some people are in relationships because they want someone to control. Some are in relationships because they are unhappy with themselves and refuse to face their unhappiness. They even have children with people they constantly dump their unhappiness on. Lust is not only sexual, but also a strong unhealthy and unmanageable desire for a person or thing. Some people are in relationships for money, power, or social posturing. When the desired outcome of a relationship is not mutually beneficial, it is problematic, and I want to make that clear!

I'M A WORK IN PROGRESS

A **CHIEVING A HEALTHY** relationship is no accident, but is the result of grueling work. Men and women committed to doing the hard work of showing vulnerability, forgiving their past, receiving inner healing, and even confessing their desire for a relationship will unlock levels of achievement. Ask your partner this question, "What do you want this relationship to accomplish?" Don't react, just listen! What did you hear? Did you hear that they want your relationship to shine on social media? Let me guess, they want arm candy and you're perfect for the job! Did you hear that they want the relationship to renew their hope in finding forever love? Did you hear that they want your relationship to make you both better people? Be honest with what you heard or didn't hear. I encourage you to not overreact to the answer. I want you to achieve clarity in your relationship. We have tried to skirt around the responsibility of achieving clarity because we're afraid it will cost us the enjoyment of the relationship. It's all fun and games until a partner wants to know their place in your life! Rightfully so, serious relationships are just that- serious! We settle for less than we desire at the cost of clarity and because we don't want to hear a disappointing truth our partner may share; we avoid asking questions altogether. This is true for men and women and simply part of the human condition. For example, a couple who should be getting to know each other but is refusing to ask probing questions are bringing past relational trauma into this budding romance. Inevitably, the new romance will look like the last and each partner will leave the connection unfulfilled while feeling unloved. But what would happen if men and women took more time to discover each other instead of only what they like about each other? Sure, you may like them and certain aspects of who they are, but who are they as a whole? What emotional baggage follows them into every relationship? Are they willing to unpack it for you? That's just a small sampling of the pertinent conversations with the power to unlock levels of emotional intimacy missing in our relationships. This also indicates the most commonly missed signs daters avoid before opting into a relationship with no future. Doing the work of discovery will not only equip daters with pertinent information, but it will also empower each of them to make an informed decision about their level of interest and the future of their relationship.

I have a very loving family and I know they love me, but sometimes family love isn't enough. I have a longing for companionship that kinship doesn't provide. I want love from outside my family dynamic and I'm OK with confessing that. When you don't have it or get it from a desired person outside of family there's tremendous pain and angst that comes along with that empty space. Many of us live in turmoil because our desires are unfulfilled. We settle for relationships that are self-serving. They drain us of our energy, and we leave depleted and injured. I know this firsthand. I fell in love with a man who didn't want me, but he wanted what I could do for him. And nothing I ever did for him, big or small, was going to be good enough. I just wanted to feel loved and be wanted by him, but that was too much to ask. I became tired. Love doesn't have to come with limitations. Being in relationships where the quality of love is tainted, or the investment of interest or attention is lacking can become toxic and dysfunctional. For years this was a struggle for me, but I finally learned to see my self-worth, while doing the necessary self-care. I also see my true value and appreciate what I bring to the table! I'm no longer willing to settle for less than what I desire. I'm at a place in my life where I'm financially stable, successful, and happy, but missing that special someone to come home to and spend quality time with. Without this, not even all the money and success matter. There is a void in my life, but I have an idea of what I want to fill it with. God first, the enjoyment of my career, my purpose and someone to share life with. Nothing else will fill that void and I won't settle for any unsatisfactory substitutions. I often ask myself why I've been in this place for so long, but you know there's work to be done internally before you're truly ready to welcome someone into your life. I don't see myself being single for the rest of my life. I want to start my own family, and like most, enjoy our unique traditions and special days throughout the year. Lately I've found myself asking God to show me the purpose of this weight. Sometimes I get lonely and tempted to try and force something, but I'm learning to appreciate the process. I must be patient. In making that decision, I'm saving time by not just dating anyone. I'm not a serial dater, I want to find my person and just be happy. I don't need anyone bringing any extra problems or pain into my life as I work on myself. I think that's the real explanation for me and my dating life right now, I'm a work in progress.

DOING THE WORK

ONCE YOU LEAN into the necessary work of affecting change in your life, you're not only a work in progress, but you're also a worker in progress! For some of us, therapy may be a part of the work but we may also need lower intensity activities like a walk in the park or reading a book. Healing while learning to love yourself is key to a great relationship which will make you a much better romantic partner and friend. Yes, we want to be in a relationship, but what are you willing to sacrifice so that your relationship lasts? Are you willing to sacrifice to the point of being single while you do the necessary work? Too often, we try to build relationships with structural flaws in the foundation that can't support the weight of the house. In That house is one for which we we're other instances, we find faulty construction in the tools we use (love vs. lust), and even the materials used (materialism, sexism, etc.) I want to let you know that the best construction is built on a firm foundation of love and requires as much demolition as it does construction. What will you have to unlearn to be a better romantic partner? What learned behaviors will you be forced to dismantle for the sake of future relationships? What inside of you needs to be built up so that you refuse to accept the bare minimum and enforce accountability in your relationships? What should you be doing to vastly improve the quality of your relationships going forward? Invest in yourself so that you have more substantial dividends to contribute to the success of your relationship.

> *"When two people intentionally work toward*
> *a purposeful relationship as a common*
> *goal, the relationship is so easy."*
> CHANEL N. SCOTT

There is a benefit to doing the work together. Once you complete the assignment on yourself and collaborate with your partner, tremendous results can be achieved by your synergy. The hardest part of your journey to healing will be to forget your past. You may not be able to erase the memory, but you must do the work to remove it from your relationship. It will take time but learn to eliminate the triggers that evoke destructive memories and subsequent behaviors in your relationship. Remember, this work is a team lift and can only be accomplished by two people committed to it. If your partner is toxic and unwilling, your relationship may never progress and may even succumb to the toxicity and poison you both spew out towards one another. This is why it's so important to develop healthy communication habits. Most analogies of teamwork are derived from sports, but have you ever seen a marching band moving in sync? They're on the same field seemingly riding the same wavelength and moving at the same cadence. The sound you hear isn't only harmonious, it's poetry in motion! Have you analyzed the sound of your relationship? It's going to take hard work to get on the same accord.

EXTRACTING YOUR EMOTIONS

EMOTIONS PLAY A vital role in the health of our relationships. Oxford English Dictionary defines emotions as, *"a natural instinctive state of mind deriving from one circumstance, mood or relationship with others."* Emotions release a chemical reaction in our brain based on the way we feel. Love is an action word, but what we feel as love is an emotion. In a relationship, emotions are expressed as joy, love, fear and even anger. When expressed negatively, our emotional response can leave a lasting, damaging effect on the relationship.

> *"I'm led by my emotions, especially if I'm passionate about something. I've grown accustomed to it and it's extremely hard for me not to."*
> CHANEL N. SCOTT

Emotional awareness (knowing what I feel and why) helps me learn about myself and build good relationships. Exercising emotional integrity leads my interactions with my friends, family, and a romantic partner. One of the provocative triggers for me is the feeling of being ignored. You read earlier in the book about how I responded as a younger woman who didn't feel seen, heard, or valued. At my height, I'm hard to miss but being made to feel like I'm only a few inches tall elicited some of the most toxic interactions I can remember! No one should ever be made to feel this way and should never treat that feeling like it's something normal. Be aware, there's only so much a person can take before they explode! I'm an overthinker and regularly tend to consider only the worst possible outcomes in situations. As much as I try to change this, I sometimes struggle to clear the lens of negative past experiences. This is also an indication of the deep-seated pain in need of healing to erase the pain of my past. For years I had no trustworthy outlet, so I created a pattern of protection that internalized my feelings for fear of rejection. There is no greater pain than your feelings being used against you. I made a habit of shutting down and internalizing my feelings. I thought I was protecting myself from an attack on my vulnerability but all those years it was like a weapon internally wreaking havoc on my sensibilities. The danger in trying to shield yourself from the reaction to your feelings is that there's nothing or no one there to shield you from yourself. The damage is implosive not explosive, but the damage inflicted hurts everyone involved. I've been there before, once you feel you've had enough and can't take it anymore, you're all over the place! Imagine letting a balloon go, it flies all over the place only deflating and moving erratically through the air with no destination in mind. I have dealt with people who have pushed me to the point of what I would described as volcanic eruption. These eruptions were so destructive, and there was no way for me to deny responsibility for the damage caused.

I couldn't continue this way. Medical science says that we shouldn't because of its adverse effect on our bodies. I no longer put energy into situations that don't have a direct impact on my life. Now when I'm offended or my feelings get hurt, my response is determined by the impact of the situation it plays in my life rather than the actual offense. Some situations should be handled privately, but others need to be dealt with at the same moment and place of the offense. The reason for this isn't confrontational, it's practical.

When you let time pass, many people tend to forget and have to be reminded of their offense. By this time, they no longer remember or identify with the impact of the offense, making a resolution impractical and nearly impossible. For instance, I no longer allow people to treat me differently in the presence of others. If you are in my life, understand that I live by consistency. The consistency I give is what is expected in return. No more giving the benefit of the doubt, my expectations are clear so be intentional with your respect because I will be intentional about resisting disrespect. I hid my true emotions for years and kept things that were offensive to me bottled up. I didn't want them to know how I was feeling and certainly didn't want them to know that I felt that way because of them. My emotional integrity was compromised because I forced myself to interact in ways that were disingenuous, and I was "fake" because of a fear of their hypothetical response. I didn't know how they would respond and never gave them a chance to because I "solved it" by concealing my true feelings. I doubted whether or not it was worth mentioning because of the fear that my feelings would be exploited or worse, that they would be used against me. I was worried about being received in the right manner or if my approach was even palatable. This was a normal occurrence when trying to process my thoughts, and emotions. I've always tried to be considerate of others, but over time, this consideration led to the misappropriation of my feelings. What should have provided leverage or created balance in the relationship became a weight and destroyed any semblance of balance. I was uncertain about broaching sensitive subjects and issues, instead I found peace in a lack of communication. I didn't want to be a burden. I just wanted to enjoy the relationship as much as I enjoyed the person or so I thought. I was the only one not enjoying the relationship because there was no resolution to the emotional void I felt.

One coping mechanism I discovered that served me well was detachment. In relationships, we seldom think about it, but we've all done it. You know, the break off before the breakup! The people closest to me get the truest, most vulnerable version of me, but they also get a fearless version of me. This version of me is unafraid to prove a point or reinforce my position in their life. We should never have to feel unheard or ignored but sometimes, the people closest to us hurt us the easiest. I've had to endure awkward moments when faced with the reality of who I was in a person's life. A genuine fear of mine was asking where I stood with them all because of not wanting reality to smack me in the face! This is why verbal communication is important. You want to hear them say it, but don't discount what their actions are or are not saying. Many times, what they do is a clear indication of how they view you and the relationship. Rejection is bad enough on its own but, if I have to do the detective work of discovering that I'm being rejected, we've got another huge reaction coming. I'm getting better, but now I just demand clear communication to avoid any type of confusion. In my quest for clarity, I had to learn the concept of timing and how to know when to have certain conversations. In some instances, after taking a few days to reflect, I realized that the person may not know how a certain interaction made me feel. It's important to me that my feelings are taken into consideration so that I'm not always fighting to prove myself or compete with others to be part of a person's life.

"See me, don't make me feel invisible!"
CHANEL N. SCOTT

A healthy emotional response is rooted in trust. If I trust your intentions, my emotional response corresponds to that level of trust and vulnerability. My sister could tell me to shut up and I would take no offense to it because I know her heart and trust her. I know she's not being disrespectful, but without an established relationship in place my response is, "who are you talking to?" Many of our relationships have met an untimely demise because we reached places in our communication and interaction that out-paced our trust and vulnerability. This offense created tension and because of the unwillingness to apologize or a misunderstanding of why it was offensive, even the hottest burning relationships have cooled to the point of a sudden breakup. Overreactions are also to blame. By misinterpreting harmless banter and inside joke or even expressed displeasure, our emotional responses have had tragic results. You can probably name a time when an emotional response was to blame for a breakup. I don't want us to rid our relationships of emotions or emotional responses, it's impera-tive that we increase our expressive intellect so that our ensuing decisions are better informed, and we have an increased commit-ment to communication in our relationships. Communication and understanding are key, you will never fully understand some-one who refuses to communicate. With growth, you discover the need to check your emotions, sit down and talk. Some of the hard conversations in relationships involve forgiving each other. Your willingness to forgive and be forgiven when you are at fault will heal you on every level in your life.

GIVE THE GIFT OF FORGIVENESS

FORGIVENESS? YOU CAN forget that! After experiencing hurt, betrayal, and even rejection in a relationship, jaded lovers often find themselves in cycles of loneliness, broken relationships, and prolonged singleness. Mending a broken heart is one thing but repairing a hole in your soul is another much more important aspect of life. The root of your relationship woes could go back further than you could imagine. If you expect to enjoy a healthy relationship, you must also expect to forgive and be forgiven! Each type of relationship comes with the expectation of forgiveness. Let's talk about the role of forgiveness in healthy relationships. The Merriam-Webster dictionary defines forgiveness as, "*the act of forgiving; to stop feeling anger towards someone; to stop feeling anger about something; to forgive someone for something wrong.*" By definition, forgiveness is a release of feelings and the harm inflicted. It very well may be that what many of us consider to be forgiveness isn't forgiveness at all. I'm not quite sure what we should call it but if you have "forgiven" a person and can't hold them harmless for what they've done, you may need to reconsider the forgiveness you have offered them. Remember true forgiveness absolves a person of not only what they've done but releases your feelings about it. We should also consider that the best forgiveness comes with personal perspectives. You may struggle with forgiveness because someone has done the unthinkable towards you, but once you're in their shoes, forgiveness may come a little easier.

Whether the person in need of forgiveness is a romantic partner, friend, family member or a stranger, forgiveness is an act of courage and benevolence that will benefit all involved. You may not know this, but forgiveness is mutually beneficial. Forgiving others will help them forgive themselves. Many times, the people in need of forgiveness become resigned to the offending behavior and remain stuck in that mindset or behavior pattern until we, by truly forgiving them, free them to again expect better of themselves and aspire to achieve it. Forgiveness isn't just giving a person another chance; it is also empowering them to do better. This is why most often; forgiveness is achieved after a relationship has ended and the offender is no longer in a position to hurt their romantic partner.

Another element of textbook forgiveness is faith. You have to believe that your heart will be protected when you release the emotional trauma inflicted on you by that person. You have to trust that you will be OK and that they will have learned their lesson when you forgive them. I've done many hard things in my lifetime, but this is probably the hardest thing to do! Imagine you forgiving someone, and they do it again. Imagine you forgive and it becomes a pattern in your relationship and the cycle of forgiving and offending begins. At what point in time do you establish parameters of acceptable behavior? We'll talk about boundaries in the next chapter, but you cannot accept cyclical behavior that tarnishes your self-image and devalues your self-worth. You deserve love that gives without taking. If that's not what you're experiencing why not change that? Yes, the Bible tells us to forgive 70x7 but on average we will never reach an instance of 490 times with a single person. Maybe if you continually recount what happened, but most of us aren't in that dire need of forgiveness from a single person. I think it's also fair to say what forgiveness isn't. Forgiveness doesn't always serve to preserve the relationship impacted by the offense. Forgiveness can take the feelings of hurt and anger away, but it may not take away the impact of the offense. This is what some families explain in their impact statement, they may be truly forgiving, but are ultimately unwilling to absolve them from the penalty of jail time. In other words, I forgive you, but you still have to pay for the crime. In relationships, forgiveness may not be enough to save it and keep you together. I want to introduce another word that accompanies forgiveness- forward. Forgiveness illuminates a pathway forward that may or may not include the offender. In this instance, we have to account for the desire that may have also been impacted by the offense. "I forgive you, but I no longer want to be with you!" is perfectly fine. However, "I forgive you but in order to regain my trust, we need time apart," is a sentence that is probably not in our lexicon. We must learn how to protect ourselves and every prospect for a healthy relationship by learning to avoid remaining connected to people who need our absence to heal and grow.

For me, once I'm past the emotional phase of the offense, the forgiveness phase begins. Once in the forgiveness phase, I'm able to gain a greater perspective of the situation or circumstance and see the bigger picture. I look at the available lessons and try to learn from each of them. In the process, I discovered their purpose and have learned that some of the lessons were only learned after repetition. I also tried to see how certain things came to be and deduce any part that I may have played in this situation. I rely on God to show me the truth about it and as He reveals the "why," I'm comforted by His presence guiding me through it. Through my natural lens, I can't see the pathway of forgiveness. I won't forgive nor will I forget. As I said earlier, forgiveness is a faith filled process that is nearly impossible without it.

> *"I Chanel don't have the strength; I have to lean on*
> *God. He has to infuse me with his strength, that's*
> *why I remain a student of the Word of God."*
> CHANEL N. SCOTT

Unconditional forgiveness is often desired and godly forgiveness is the best example of that. However, accepting forgiveness without accountability is reckless, even mindless behavior. No responsible adult in a romantic partnership should expect forgiveness to be offered with no showing of responsibility for their actions. They also have to hold themselves accountable and show through words and actions that it won't happen again. In this case what is desired isn't forgiveness but convenient amnesia. This happens when a person places the work of forgiving and forgetting on the person they offended. Remember, we're supposed to be working together here! Why can't they do the work of helping me forget the negative by making new positive memories? See, I used to hold grudges, but the lingering pain only kept me stuck in the past. I love people and want to forgive them and move forward, but the enemy makes it hard. He keeps the same old sad song playing in our minds triggering memories of hurt and anger that impede the process of and progress otherwise made by forgiving.

> *"You don't forget, but love covers*
> *a multitude of sin, right?"*
> CHANEL N. SCOTT

You may never forget how you were wronged, but it is imperative that you free yourself from the power it may hold over you.

Love covers a multitude of sins so that the fellowship is not broken. I told you that forgiveness is a faith filled tenant of healthy relationship maintenance. You place some faith in that person to not hurt you again, but you must also place your faith in God to allow him to heal, repair or restore what has been broken. I understand that some offences leave relationships irretrievably broken, but if you have agape love like God has for us, your wish for them is good even if you are no longer together. What is the value of that experience? An easy answer for most of us is that such a negative experience teaches us to never allow someone to harm us in that way ever again. If anything is worth remembering, the pain from that realization should be reflected upon as a benchmark for loyalty and respect in relationships. You know it like I do, we have tolerated less than what we deserved and expected, and it only opened the door for betrayal, abuse, and unfathomable pain in our lives. Do you honestly think that any of that is worth the experience again? That's why you remember, so you can recognize it! We all make mistakes and some of our genuine mistakes were judged too harshly or as if they were intentional, based on someone's past experiences. Most people do what they know and only learn at the level their actions are held accountable to. Life is all about experience and lessons, so hopefully as you discover lessons from the experience you're releasing the effects of the offense, no longer holding it over their head. Free them and free yourself, even if it means cutting ties. People who value you don't intend to hurt you. We are human and will inadvertently cause harm to those we love, but if you love someone, you won't be OK seeing them hurting because of you or anyone else. If you cause pain, seek to make it right and earn forgiveness from those you've hurt. Healthy relationships are no accident but are the result of hard work by two purpose-minded people! When the effort is not reciprocated, it may be time to enforce boundaries and redefine a person's role in your life.

ESTABLISHING HEALTHY BOUNDARIES

A MAJOR HALLMARK OF healthy relationships is the boundaries you set. Boundaries control what comes in and goes out and when you consider how outside forces can easily and negatively influence their relationship, it's easy to understand the necessity for boundaries. More importantly, healthy boundaries between two partners reinforce the agreed upon boundaries for the relationship. Respect, safety, trust, accountability and support all work to fortify the strength, safety and security of a relationship and our underlying tenets of a healthy one as well. It can be difficult to set parameters, but you need to. Unhealthy boundaries seek to subjugate, exert control, project distrust, insecurity and overall undermine the bond you seek to establish in your relationship. Your view of boundaries greatly impacts your relationship. If you view boundaries as restrictive, you will constantly battle the urge to breach them. However, when viewed as protective, your relationship finds safety in the clearly defined parameters of what a healthy relationship looks like to you and your partner. For the sake of your relationship, learn to set healthy boundaries and take ownership of the boundaries you set. Setting healthy boundaries begins with healthy communication. When you clearly communicate your wants, needs, likes, and dislikes, you give your relationship a great opportunity to flourish. Our excitement over new and fresh connections often impedes the boundary setting process. We flock to superficial elements of the relationship, glossing over potential red flags and resigning ourselves to mere trial and error as opposed to establishing well thought out and clearly defined parameters.

"Setting healthy boundaries starts with clear communication and the intentionality."
CHANEL N. SCOTT

Intentionality is another force behind healthy boundaries. With a clear understanding of your intentions in the relationship, everyone is clear about their desires, their pathway to them and even the purpose for them. Far too often, we choose to assume and opt into an extremely dangerous guessing game! If you opted into the guessing game, why be mad when you find out you played yourself? Many relationships succumb to the toxicity brought on by ignorance. You know you should probably inquire about people, places, and scenarios, but you choose not to, and in lieu of learning, you enjoy the false sense of peace and companionship powered by your willful ignorance. This trait is more than likely a protective measure deployed by a person whose heart has been broken and whose trust has been compromised in the worst way. Choosing not to know a person while spending time with them and growing romantically is toxic. It's destructive and can harm a person deeply. The beginning phase of a relationship is the best time to have hard talks. In theory, there will never be a good time for your partner to share bad news about them. You will also establish communication patterns and safety zones for truth telling during these earlier conversations. Boundaries aren't in place in response to past relational failures, they were put in place to enforce the pursuit of success in your current relationship.

If the information shared in the discovery process makes you uncomfortable, give yourself and your partner the freedom to step back and even pause the pursuit of the relationship. Taking necessary time to reflect, process and decompress gives you the best chance to fully understand what was said. Be fair in your handling of such sensitive information and try not to judge what you don't completely understand. This discovery phase establishes healthy communication habits and if you can't see it through in the beginning, don't expect it to change as your relationship progresses. Understand that you nor your partner are perfect and there must be a level of acceptance and accountability at play to secure the love and respect at the center of your relationship. Partners should also be willing to be held accountable to the established boundaries. Many times, we enter relationships before we are completely healed and need the cooperation of our new partner to fully manifest the needed healing. If you are in such a situation, be mindful of the sensitivity and consider the emotional toll of any potentially adverse actions. If not, you're bound to hear, "we need to set some boundaries!" or, "why would you do or say that knowing what I've already gone through?" Those words are never uttered in healthy moments, but in moments of serious conflict. When a violation of a set boundary happens, conversations should also happen. Unfortunately, these conversations are reactive and not proactive which may have precluded this breach of confidence. Clear intentions are communicated through transparent conversations and help us avoid confusion because without clarity we can't see where we are going.

Established boundaries can work as a compass for romantic partners. Not only can we see where we're going, but also ensure that we get there together! I address boundary breaches directly and then wait for feedback. I want to know how it happened, how you feel about it and your commitment to not doing it again. I make it clear that a boundary was crossed so that there is no guessing about it. I've learned that some people have different versions or definitions, but for me it comes down to respect. I give respect and expect to receive it in return. This is why even in communicating an issue with boundaries, it should be done respectfully. I'm going to communicate it, so please listen to me and consider what I have to say. I don't like being hung up on. I know some people don't care, but for me in that moment I feel like you're inhibiting me in so many ways. None of us like to feel inhibited and being forced to deny our feelings is damaging to the relationship we seek to enjoy. You can tell me that there's a better time to discuss the issue, or to give you time. I try to always provide that freedom. This way, we both try to communicate how we feel and gain a real understanding in order to move forward, together. Again, we do this together! But to deny the relationship, open and honest communication is like trying to snuff out a growing fire. Without oxygen the fire will subside, but with a steady flow of oxygen, the fire will grow and consume its subject. If the embers of our love will ever grow to consume us, we have to provide ample oxygen and let it breathe! The building blocks of the airflow is the mutual respect required to keep lines of communication open. In this digital age many messages have gone awry because text messages and emails lack the emotional expression of the human voice. If it's important to me, I'm picking up the phone to talk about it because it's important to not only communicate topics but also to use the properly intended tone.

Some of you experience anxiety when expressing yourself so texting may help break the ice and create a pathway to communicating difficult topics. Still, I prefer phone calls or in-person conversations. It's hard to misconstrue what is audibly communicated so to keep drama to a minimum, I'm dialing you up! It's important to hear the emotion behind a thought or conversation because that clarity alone can heal or destroy a relationship. This chapter helps you set and appreciate boundaries in your relationship. By developing an appreciation for them, I hope you also develop the confidence to confront the barriers to establishing healthy boundaries in your relationship.

> *"I don't spend time with people I don't like, I don't do casual dating at all!"*
> CHANEL N. SCOTT

I don't spend time with people I don't like, nor do I casually date. Some people do it because they're lonely or just want company. I'm not judging them, but I am very selective about who my time and life is spent with. I expect that exclusivity to be rewarded with intentionality. It's obvious when a connection has been made because our time together is not aimless. We have already crossed the threshold of "like" and are extracting the value gained from our time together. Why mess that up by crossing established boundaries and potentially harming the relationship? There are some boundary breaches in my past that were so devastating that it sent me into a state of singleness. I never thought that I'd emerge from this lonely abyss. Unresolved relationship trauma lingers and impacts future relationships and prospects, but you don't have to let it. For some of you, the most important boundary is to keep the past in the past- where it belongs.

REMOVE YOURSELF FROM LOVE ROOTED IN REJECTION

U NREALISTIC EXPECTATIONS LEAD to let-downs. Trying to love someone who doesn't want your love, companionship or partnership will only hurt you in the end. Unfortunately, when the relationship ends, the grief is so compounded that it affects every part of who you are. This existential rejection has made future relationships impossible and now made the lovelorn impervious to any new expression of love in romantic partnerships. You deserve love that comes with acceptance and not rejection. Words and actions will prove it so we must do the work of understanding how our lover is not only communicating acceptance, but rejection as well. This awareness may cause pain, but the freedom gained to love and to be loved with acceptance will heal any broken heart. Accepting rejection is difficult but opens a door to greater possibilities in love and the greatest love of all, yourself. Rejection sometimes comes as a protection of the lover's heart. When rejection comes as a protection of their peace, the rejected have to consider their ways. Sometimes, it's too little too late and other times, the effort a lover pleaded for came when the flame flickered out and long after the thrill of love was gone. What can you do when this happens? The only thing left to do at this point is for the rejected party to work on one's self. Many times, we reject our romantic partners because of the lingering effects of rejection in our own lives.

In relationships, be wary of the manifestation of what I call a **rejection without separation** (this is not a clinical term, but an observation). In this manifestation, rejection doesn't immediately materialize as a separation, though the rejection lasts until the dissolution of a marriage or relationship. We are accustomed to rejection that leads to a separation but the psychological effects don't directly sever the platonic or romantic connection and can be quite traumatic. The weight of this trauma becomes existential as you seek to rationalize the rejection and unjustly find fault within yourself. The struggle to understand why you or aspects of your behavior or personality are rejected can also cause tremendous mental strain. Like many rejected people in romantic relationships, there is a refusal without disposal. This common practice of rejection refuses everything but the romantic connection.

Something within the connection is lifeless and we can't figure out how or why! In this instance, the rejector continues and possibly even intensifies their rejection while maintaining the connection with the rejected. In other words, they're doing enough to keep you around so that they can continue rejecting you or aspects of who you are. This isn't only confusing, it's disrespectful. It's so frustrating, it makes you want to ask, "if you don't want me, why are you still with me?" This damaging dilemma has harmed friendships, families, business partnerships, and romantic relationships. Though this behavior is confusing, it is also quite common. Many of us have been made the butt of jokes among friends and family to later be told the rejector was *"just playing."* Some of us have endured this gaslighting to only be told that we're taking life too seriously or reading too much into the situation. If we think about it, the only bullying some of us have endured has come at the hands of those we called friends, loved ones, or lovers.

The motivation varies, but most often this behavior is meant to cover a hole in the soul. In some capacity, it helps them love themselves better. For some, this toxicity is the only way they know how to express "love." For others, they're rejecting your love because they don't know how to be loved or struggle to resolve their need for a connection with their disbelief that they are deserving of love. Then, there's the plain old narcissist who doesn't view you as worthy of their love or companionship, and instead of love, they act to subjugate and demean you.

One of the roots of rejection is the lack of emotional availability. The one we desire or even the one we love may be physically present, but emotionally detached. We try and try to make a lasting connection, yet nothing happens. Why? We're making memories and may even be making babies but no actual connection. This part of rejection hurts the worst because it's deep. It's so deep, that it doesn't even feel like rejection. It feels like we have to work harder, think harder, and ultimately find a way to receive the love we're giving. Songs like, "I'm gonna Make You Love Me," and quotes like, "All my life I had to fight to prove my love to you," have normalized struggle love, but how can you make someone love you? A person who lacks emotional availability has denied the outside world access to their deepest vulnerability.

Time can undo this but, in the instance when it doesn't, you've only wasted time. What can open the door of emotional availability when a person has guarded their vulnerability like the gold at Fort Knox? How can you create desire when desire isn't well...desired? Another song that communicates emotional intelligence and awareness says, "I can't make you love me if you don't." Sometimes, it's not you and the other person may not realize that it's them. Emotional unavailability causes that rejection and may have been passed down from parent to child and from former lovers. It's a reach but, the lack of emotional availability may even be considered a trauma response. How do you make sense of potential mates who remain guarded but enter the dating pool, anyway? Overwhelmingly, those hurt people are the ones who over time hurt other people.

Rejection and the emotional trauma it causes doesn't preclude us from love and marriage. Instead, the malignant manifestation has the potential to wreck even our most valued relationships when we least expect it. If we refuse to address the emotional trauma experienced as a rejected child, friend, or lover, we will inevitably project it onto those we've committed to love.

Our relationships deserve emotional intelligence which requires self-awareness. As stated before, we have all been on both sides of rejection and it doesn't feel good. So many times, we fight rejection because of its emotional impact. None of us want to feel rejected because it most often leads to a dark place and, recovery can sometimes be a long time coming. Rejection is often re-direction. Once you get over your feelings, you can often see a better path forward whether a job, love interest, friend, church, business, or other entity. While it's unhealthy to resist rejection, there's health in the resistance to the negative feeling rejection brings. Is there such a thing as a healthy response to rejection?

With this in mind, we encourage emotional healing. Get healed in your soul so that you love and receive love from a place of purity. The road to recovery may be long and daunting, don't let that discourage your journey to pursue love. The self-care involved may be arduous and the disconnections it causes may be demanding, but it's well worth the work. You deserved to be loved as a whole person and we hope you understand that there are people in the world capable of that. You do not have to settle for love from a person refusing to love you wholly, nor do you have to try and love a person who can't be loved fully. Put your whole self into love and if that requires removing yourself from people, friends, or lovers who can't love all of you, *"take your whole self out!"* As you go forward and embrace new friends and potential partners, love with purity and learn to reject any semblance of platonic or romantic relationships with rejection at its root!

WHAT IT MEANS TO ME

R ELATIONSHIPS THRIVE WITH respect. If you want to see a relationship fail fast, infuse it with disrespect. I have seen this happen time and time again, men and women treat each other like trash because they disrespect them, their perspective, and their person. If you truly respect a person, you have regard for them. What this means is that you think about them and their well-being when you make decisions about you, them, and the relationship. You also consider their feelings when making decisions that may not directly impact them. Because of their proximity to you, you understand that any decision you make will indirectly affect them, so you make wise decisions in consideration of them.

A friend of mine told me about a big fight he and his wife had when she came home late from work and told the kids to do the opposite of what he had told them to do, moments earlier. The kids didn't think anything about what he said because they wanted to do what their mother said. This blew up because he felt like she disrespected him, even after he told her that he told them to do what they were doing. As parents, this is a tricky situation because sometimes, they have different ideas about children and child-rearing. While the man wants to enforce structure, the mother wants to explore individuality and freedoms. There is room for both, but it doesn't happen by accident. My friend felt that his wife disregarded his instructions and worse, disrespected him as a man, her husband, and their children's father. What do you think? Was this an overreaction, or did he have the latitude to make a fuss about it?

I don't know the dynamics of their relationship, but I can tell you that respect is not something that happens without effort. Respect is something you give, so you can imagine that there are things we do that erode the respect and regard we have for one another. I won't get into that yet, but I do want to make you aware that your relationship will never grow beyond the level of respect you have for one another. Think about it, what will keep you from entertaining another person? It should be common decency to not do anything secret that would harm the relationship, right? Well, we're in a new day where too many relationships are open by default because people don't respect themselves enough to be bound to a single person. I'm not talking about polyamory, most of those couples are poly of their own volition.

But, if you have a partner, you should respect them enough to consider them and their feelings. You should also respect their boundaries. I get it, sometimes the people in our lives project hurt and anger in the enforcement of boundaries, but that's not in every case. Sometimes, people are explaining their tolerance or lack of tolerance for certain behaviors when defining their boundaries. Respect goes a long way. Even if your partner isn't doing what you would like for them to do, you can respectfully redirect them. They're not children, they're a responsible adult which should make the redirection easier. If they don't, you can also respectfully remove yourself from the relationship.

We've all seen examples of men and women who bring family and friends too closely to the relationship. They're on the phone telling them everything, posting every little tidbit on social media, and worse, bring them along when you would prefer an intimate outing between you two. Where's the respect there? There is none and apparently, there are no boundaries, either. Respect is a mutual consideration. Think of it like this, "How am I considering what this person perceives as respect/disrespect?" I have another friend who got mad that her husband paid all the bills late. She paid them the day the notice came in, but he paid them days before disconnection on the regular. Worse yet, he would be the one talking about spending though he waited until the last possible minute to pay the bills. Whenever she complained about it, he would always reply, "but I paid it!"

I don't think this will ever get solved, but respect can foster an understanding. He does pay the bills before disconnected but not when it would make his wife comfortable enough to trust him. That's something to think about, isn't it? He's comfortable but she's not. How would you start that conversation? After bringing it up several times, you know it's going to lead to an argument, so it just flies under the radar until you see the past due notice, again.

Tone indicates respect but there will come a time when tone gets tossed out the window! Without respect, we have nothing! If you don't respect me enough to hear me, we've got a major problem! I'm sure you're wondering, yes, I have my friend's permission to share these stories. When I began writing this book, I wanted to present as many possibilities as I could to help mold relationships into the best possible iteration of a loving, caring, respectful and respectable union. This doesn't happen without hard work and sometimes, we have to face the ugly parts of who we are to get there.

How do we get there? Today, you don't have to read a map, the GPS talks to you. "Turn here, exit there, keep straight, make a U-Turn," and more are all directions communicated by the GPS in our cars and on our phones. It's no different in relationships, communication will lead you to the best place in your relationships. Communication will also define what is respect and disrespect. Many times, this communique happens after an event, argument, or as an aversion to them. Either way, this communication is a vital part of building a healthy relationship. Do you know what else healthy communication makes room for? The truth! When my friend took his gripe to his wife, she didn't want to hear it. Do you know what else came out in that conversation? His wife pointed to a few projects around the home that he hadn't taken attention to. To her, he had been ignoring her for months because he never acted on what she desired to change around the house.

Just like respect, communication works both ways. While you demand to be heard, you must also listen. Even when you're right, there may be something communicated that opens up understanding for both of you. Try it some time, you may like it! How did they resolve this issue of finger pointing, well, there was a reinforcement of respect and apology. But he didn't win because he still had work to do to reinforce the respect he has for his wife. If he won't do what she's asking him to or communicate where he is in the process of doing it, he's disregarding her, still. Do you get the point now? Respect is communicated. What is respect/disrespect to you may not be the same for your partner and if you disagree with it, you must also communicate that. The problem in many relationships is that we don't regard our partner enough to openly communicate with them often enough to remain connected. This may involve daily communication, check-ins about goals and desires, or other issues relative to the relationship. If you are disrespectful in a way that I have already defined, I deserve to hold you accountable for it and expect change, don't I?

Think about it, none of us are willing to disrespect ourselves on the level that others will. We've done some pretty debasing things in our lives, but most of us have a moral compass. If I allow you to develop a lifestyle of disrespecting me, it's personal disrespect by proxy. I'm disrespecting myself by allowing you to do it. That's not good but this has become the norm in relationships, today. Many of us operate without regard to our partners and we're too comfortable doing so. We don't think about them and don't consider them when making decisions of all kinds. If I respect you, I want you to be a part of what I'm a part of. I want you to have a say and I want to make you comfortable. I respect you enough to bring you along with me. This should be the bedrock of our bond as partners. We have to do some unlearning in this area, especially given the vitriol being passed as expertise on social media.

We no longer desire partners, but if you pay attention, the subconscious desire for real partnership has not gone away. We speak from hurt, and thoughts of self-preservation and not from a healthy place willing to welcome love and partnership in their truest forms. Relationships matter, but more importantly, the quality of your relationship matters the most. What good is it to have a partner if that partner adds no value to you? You have a boyfriend or girlfriend, husband, or wife but what value do they bring to your life?

Appraise your relationship and see what value they add. If you don't see that they add to your life, seek out answers that will help change that. More often than not, we will discover that a person is unyielding to change because they don't view their partner as worthy of the change. Men say it as well as women, "They'll change for the right one!" How could it be that the person you view as "the one" doesn't view you as "the right one" worth changing for?

There's a lot to unpack in that conversation, but it needs to happen. I would ask that person, what don't you trust about me that keeps you from making the changes necessary to benefit this relationship? Some people are insatiable, and no amount of change will appease them, so don't lump them into this conversation. I'm talking about well-adjusted people who have identified areas of weakness within their relationships but remain closed-minded when presented with growth opportunities.

Our relationships deserve better and though it won't be easy, it's worth it! We have fallen for what looks good on television and social media but remain oblivious to the depth of work required to achieve some resemblance of success in our relationships. If you knew how hard some couples had to work to keep it together, you would never view them as "couple goals" again. Each couple has real problems and real resistance to change! Nobody wants to become someone else for someone else! We love who we are, we love the person we've become and it's not far-fetched to think that you have it well enough together to find someone who will appreciate the person you are. But what will you do when you discover that you're just as imperfect as your partner? Even if you've done major work to get where you are, don't be surprised if there's even more work to be done for the sake of your relationship!

Pride is the culprit. We don't want to change because though we truly love our partner, we love ourselves even more. That's why respect is lacking in relationships. In this chapter, I wanted to allow you to confront the barriers preventing you from truly respecting your partner. Reflect on your relationship and appraise your respect for one another. If you can do better, commit to honoring your partner with the respect they deserve. If they need to make the change, take the conversation to them, respectfully.

This chapter helps us to understand the importance of respect in the context of your relationship. As the relationship continues to grow, communicate frequently and gain new perspectives as needed. I want you to have a healthy relationship and I look forward to hearing how you've grown after reading this book!

DO YOU HEAR YOURSELF?

COMMUNICATION IS VITAL to the health of any relationship. Whether romantic, platonic, or professional, communication is key to sustaining a viable connection with another person. Communication is a struggle in many relationships because we bring unhealthy communication practices and behaviors into new relationships. We bring the same habits that led to the breakdown of previous relationships only to find similar, chaotic outcomes. How could you expect a different outcome if you've done nothing differently? I should add that authentic communication is key. It's not enough to establish good communication because some relationships with good communication are also plagued by the problem of verbosity. Partners are either talking too much or to the wrong people about intricate matters of the relationship. We are all striving to find that "sweet spot" of communication where we can even finish each other's sentences or interpret our partner's thoughts through their actions or with a glance. Until we reach that point, we have to rely on their words to discern what they are communicating to us.

Relying merely on words handicaps relationships because words and actions should communicate a singular thought. When they don't, it's no surprise that the relationship never reaches its fullest potential. You can't let that smooth talk fool you because some people love to hear themselves talk. If you let them, they'll talk long enough that you'll start to believe them! Throughout the relationship, these people manipulate the partners they profess to love into accepting behaviors inconsistent with love. They literally talk their partners into accepting outside partners, adopting alternative lifestyles, and as we see frequently, accepting children conceived during the relationship with an outsider. We all know someone who has believed what they heard instead of what they've been shown. The proof is there, but they've chosen to take their partner's word as the truth.

Have you ever seen a relationship that leaves you wondering what keeps them together? Look no further than what is being said and believed to discover the illusion of what "looks" like a relationship. If a person says they love you but does things that suggest they don't love you, do they love you at all? You've heard it said before and I'll say it again, love is an action word. This behavior can also resemble the characteristics of a trauma bond where you find yourself in an unhealthy relationship that you can't seem to leave because there are both positive and negative reinforcements in the relationship. If you love me, you don't have to say it as much as you should do it! What is love, and how do you communicate love? There should be a clear example of how love is demonstrated in the relationship, and not merely saying, "I love you." Mere words can become so addictive that the conversation and communication component overpowers all other aspects of the relationship. This happens quite often but the best defense against this toxicity is time!

You can only hope that the manipulated partner comes to their senses and the relationship ends with them having some semblance of self-respect and a healthy desire for companionship. Most times after an excruciating heartbreak, single men and women are too jaded to be in a loving relationship. My hope for you is that you find healing and true love after overcoming the toxicity and dysfunction in your past relationships.

The purpose of this chapter is to evoke the reader to really dig deep and do some self-reflection on their own experiences in the context of their relationship. Sometimes it's good and rewarding and other times, it's repulsive and triggering. However, self-reflection allows you to become aware of your own emotions and intentions.

I want this book to help people understand relationships and ultimately, themselves. If you recognize certain adverse behaviors in yourself or your partner that provoke you to change, I've done my job. If you're a person struggling with relational woes and you're motivated to take steps to do the challenging work, even better!

Believe it or not, I've learned so much from my past relationships! As I began to write, it was hard to stop! I've had so many "aha" moments throughout the writing process. Here's one of the more profound revelations I received during the writing process that I think is worth shedding light on for those of you who may be experiencing similar behavior. Some people believe that if they talk long enough or loud enough, they will wear down your bandwidth to deal with them! Their end game is to wear you down so that you're unable to challenge them and call out their inconsistent behaviors and habits. This is a red flag from the first time it happens because if you allow it to happen once, you're permitting them to do it again! You often see this type of behavior in relationships outside of the realm of romantic relationships too. But let's put a twist on it, ladies since we're specifically talking about romantic relationships, when a man who is telling you that you're the most beautiful woman in the world while his caresses shift to unhooking your bra. Because you want to believe in the intimacy of the moment, you just may overlook the smooth operation of your guard being lowered and your defenses disarmed with each careless whisper and meaningless mumble. Deep down, you know he's pandering to that emptiness inside of you that so desperately seeks companionship and genuine love but before you know it, the moment has passed and you're just another hook-up. You've surrendered your virtue to yet another man who listlessly engaged you long enough to get what he wanted from you.

You may have toyed with the idea of it blossoming into a long-term relationship but how long can a relationship last when it's based on empty chatter? Hopefully, you soon discover that a relationship like this has no foundation. Women are guilty of this, too! Many men are undone by their unbridled lust and fall right into the hands of women who have no real desire for them and will toss them to the curb like trash on bulk pickup week! This was Samson's problem! In the Bible, Samson was a man who was chosen by God to destroy the enemies of God's people. Samson had an affinity for a certain type of woman. He liked women "over there", and he consistently chose the wrong woman. He met his match in Delilah, though. Her pillow talk game was strong! She badgered him about the source of His strength because she secretly partnered with Samson's enemies to try and destroy him. If we look back on any of our failed relationships, we'll see how our partners were talking but we weren't listening. We weren't paying attention to their actions or the lack thereof to see if they aligned with the words that were coming out of their mouth. People will reveal their true motives and may even say them directly to you! The question is, are you listening? Did you hear what you wanted to hear, or did you hear what they actually said?

When you hear it or see actions that don't match their words, you have the responsibility of challenging them. Otherwise, you become the fool they suspect you to be! This goes back to communicating shared goals and establishing boundaries in the relationship! By agreeing to the goals, we set and agree to pursue, we agree to be bound to the pursuit of these goals and to ultimately be held accountable when our actions aren't conducive to their accomplishment. So, if your partner doesn't change adverse behavioral patterns in the relationship or reject redirection, you have a responsibility to address it. When your partner doesn't do what they said they would do, why not say something? At this point, I would ask you, "didn't you hear what you said?"

This is all too common in relationships, these days. We don't say what we feel, nor do we say what needs to be said because we want to keep the "peace." It's not peace, your relationship has been compromised by fear! I'm not telling you to nag your partner, let me be clear on that. "We nag because we care!" Have you heard that, before? I know it doesn't seem that way, but it's true! We nag because we desire the security of your consistency! When we don't have it, we try to create it by forcing you to do it. It usually isn't successful, because all it does is drive a wedge between you and your partner. This unnecessary tension in the relationship between partners makes moving forward nearly impossible while the issue at the root of the nagging still goes unaddressed.

The response from inconsistent partners is baffling. I've seen the worst of it, they try to gaslight you into thinking that your normal response is an overreaction to their awful treatment and disrespect of the relationship. You don't have to take that! You've tried to be rational; you've listened to their words and watched them act out in ways that are damaging to the relationship. You're not crazy, you're traumatized! I don't like to suggest breakups, but some of us need to realize that we're with people who are detrimental to our well-being. They're detrimental to the health and stability of the relationship and it's time to pull the plug!

Communication encompasses words and actions. When words and actions are not consistent, we reserve the right to demand their alignment. Make sure that you listen to each other when you talk. Listen attentively and intently so that your behaviors are inspired by the words you hear. Also, be cognizant of what you have said so that your actions contribute to the general health and well-being of your relationship.

Lastly, mean what you say, and don't say anything you don't mean. For far too long, we have tried to put a bandage where incompatibility is hemorrhaging in our relationships. Unfortunately, once incompatibility is revealed, some of our relationships won't survive. Don't feel bad about it, some of our relationships aren't intended to be long-term and some of them should have never been a reality! When we lie to ourselves and our partners, we prolong the inevitable and by default agree to extended periods of unhappiness and unfulfillment. Tell the truth and be truthful in your actions. If you don't love a person enough to honor them in the relationship as your partner or do right by them, let them go! If you can't be who they need you to be and are unwilling to do the work to become that person, give them the gift of the opportunity to find the person who will. Furthermore, let them do this without you being a part of their life or romantic partnership perspective!

I want readers to know that healthy relationships mean the world to me, and I'm fulfilled by knowing that I'm contributing to the health of any relationship connected to me and the reading of "Relationships Matter"!

YOU'RE NOT CRAZY, YOU'RE TRAUMATIZED!

I F WE'RE HONEST with ourselves, many of us are still impacted by the trauma of our youth. Unresolved trauma manifests as poor decision making, poor communication, and inability to connect with romantic partners. It will also disturb emotional and relational deficiencies. This level of trauma also impacts the way we view ourselves and those in our lives. Reactions become overreactions and disagreements sever meaningful relationships because of the distrust and dysfunction that continuously hampers any attempt at long term relationship. Unresolved past trauma impacts the way we react to emotional triggers, they affect our relationships and how we love and receive love. Hurt people do indeed hurt people so it's important that we purge the toxicity trauma leaves behind before inadvertently subjecting those we love and intend to love to it. This work isn't easy, but it is worth it! Choosing not to heal for any reason has drastic results. At the very least, you subject others to the same kind of hurt that you experienced or worse. You simply hurt everyone in your path some kind of way. The Merriam-Webster dictionary defines trauma as "A difficult or unpleasant experience that causes someone to have mental or emotional problems usually for a long time. A disordered psychic or behavioral state resulting from severe mental or emotional stress or physical injury." Consider this definition and apply its understanding to anything that challenges healthy relationships and interactions. As we grow older, many of us will face the reality that we have been traumatized by past relationships, partners, our parents, and even the schoolyard bully. Some jobs and working environments are known to inflict trauma on its employees which create harsh work conditions. How do you move on? There is a marked difference in leaving and moving on. There may be a great struggle to leave and maybe even a crisis that forces an exodus, but that pales in comparison to the valiant effort of taking your power back when it has been taken from you. Trauma also robs us of feelings of safety, worthiness, care, and concern from those you love and trust. Yes, trauma leaves a lingering feeling of distrust because most often, trauma is inflicted on us by those we love. But you don't have to remain bound to the trauma of your past. If you still hope for healthy romantic relationships, it is very possible. This choice is the "moving on" that I mentioned earlier.

Healing begins with acceptance. Despite your disappointment, you have to accept what happened and who did it. Don't think that calling an event something else will help you through your healing process. This calls for a vulnerability that few can handle. It will involve feelings of sadness, anger, and confusion amongst many others. Understand that you perpetuate trauma when you refuse to name it. I'll start by asking a simple question, what happened? Was it infidelity in the relationship, abuse of any kind, a betrayal by a friend, abandonment, parental absenteeism? These are just a few of the betrayals that cause deep seated emotional harm and inhibit our ability to be productive in relationships, absent in friendships and devoid of any real kinship. Here's another question, who did it? What was your relationship to the person who caused you such deep pain that so negatively impacted you? Can I continue? I understand that we may be unlocking doors to many areas you have denied access to, but you deserve to be free from past trauma. Next, let's unpack how what they did hurt you! Trauma by any other name is still trauma! With instances of sexual and physical abuse, it's not hard to understand how that may impact you physiologically and mentally, but with other traumas the damage may not be as perceptible. One of the biggest misnomers after experiencing trauma is "feeling fine." "Fine" is not an indication of health and well-being. Many people who feel fine still struggle in their relationships due to untreated and unresolved trauma. Many people who felt fine days before a major medical episode were in the ICU days later while others were in the morgue, a casualty of an undiagnosed or undetectable medical issue. The life of your relationship is no different and I want it to survive the threat of any imminent yet undetectable danger. Simply put, you have to heal. You have to become better than who or what broke you. Next, I need to ask another question. What can you do about what happened? This is a profoundly serious question because it begs us to retrieve our power and perspective that was robbed by trauma. Our response to trauma is often inaction because we still see the offender in a light that doesn't match what they did to us. We never expected them to betray us like that so we're stuck trying to resolve what happened with who we always thought they would be. Let's give them a new name though, violator. They violated your trust, the relationship, friendship and possibly even your body and you no longer have to protect them. You don't even have to protect the relationship violated by their actions. Now, any action taken is done against the violator; whether they were an ex, family member, frenemy, coworker, neighbor... anyone! Now let's try and answer the question of what you can do about it. This is a compound issue because the real trauma of the situation may lie in understanding what you should have already done or what should have already happened. Should you have deleted them from your social media channels and block them from future access to you? Should you have deleted their number from your phone contacts? Are you processing guilt for not filing a police report when you were physically or sexually assaulted? If so, achieving healthy relationships also requires us to exercise the regret we carry with us. Many of us struggle to enjoy healthy relationships because we can't see a future without regret minimizing our efforts to love and be loved. You may have harmed someone in a relationship and are carrying guilt. If so, have you sought help to ensure it never happens again? Remember, healthy romantic partners allow themselves to be held accountable. Be willing to show off your progress but if you know that you haven't done the work, that should be your only focus! What happened is in the past and you have to rely on your self-worth to see a path forward.

What a lot of us have chosen to do instead is operate in a spirit of co-dependency. In lieu of healing, we rely on the whole parts of another person to fill the void in our lives. We have taken the phrase "you complete me" to heart in the worst possible way. This will also explain why relationships sour. If you rely on another person to complete you but have nothing to offer them in your completeness or their love tank is depleted because of the continual deposits into yours, this failure should come as no surprise. The relationship is still off balance because only one person is "complete" but not whole. We spend years searching for someone to love us as we are instead of doing the work to perfect who and what we could be. This codependency is toxic because the behavior is parasitic at its absolute best. This happens in friendships and romantic partnerships alike and almost always ends with dire outcomes. There are times when this pattern gets us into more trouble than we were in before the connection because we link up with people who prey on the emptiness in our lives. Healing from trauma will restore your perspective to a healthy and safe outlook and valuable relationships. Some of us project unrealistic expectations on those we're in relationships with and end up hurting ourselves more when they don't meet them. Other times the conflict in fallout is so severe that we leave the relationship more jaded than we were when it began. You are responsible for your healing and no one else. This doesn't mean that you shut others out, but it does mean that you take the lead in doing the work. We will always need people in our lives, that's a basic human need. You're reading this book because of your interest in learning about what matters in a relationship so there's the most important part. You need people, we weren't meant to do this life alone, it's impossible! What we may need to do is heal broken parts of us so that we can put people in their proper places in our lives! You'll find that healing may be impossible because you're too close to the people who hurt you or continue hurting you. This level of co-dependency is best defined as trauma bonding. In this next chapter I want to share a story about a trauma bond that left me in extreme pain. I had just cycled through a relationship held together by a trauma bond, but I knew it was time to stop that wild ride!

BREAKING THE BONDS OF TRAUMA

IN THE FIRST show of our debut season on Fox Soul, we discovered that trauma bonding may not be what we have known it to be. Our show on the topic revealed the truth about the bond created between the person inflicting trauma and their victim. As the panelists shared their stories, weights were lifted in the room. We don't often stop to think about it, but celebrities face the same issues that everyday people face, and their freedom can help you reach your freedom faster and with clarity! This is the CheMinistry experience! Freeing yourself from the bonds of trauma is an intentional act. You have to decide that you have suffered long enough! Break the chain and free yourself from the bonds of trauma without delay! It was a relationship, a situationship and entanglement all at the same time. I spent a few years in a relationship with a man who just couldn't bring himself to choose me, and I lived to talk about it. Initially, I thought we had a common bond but that's not what it was. I actually think he was afraid of committing himself to one woman. He didn't try too hard to address it, he just did enough to give off the impression that he was trying. We know men and women like that, don't we? They come into our lives, or we allow them into our lives in a state of readiness to begin a romantic relationship but without a plan of commitment. I entertained this man longer than I should have. Truth is, he was never as into me as I was him, but when everyone else knows what you're next to learn, you'll find that amazing person is actually a fraud. The man I had my sights set on was emotionally unavailable. Now, if I was willing to give him my body, he would have gladly taken it. Money and anything else I was willing to give would have also been freely received. Can you imagine? These men come into women's lives with the prospect of enhancing their own, but only tear down the self-esteem they've built up and destroying the self-worth they finally come to understand. Many women are broken because of this. By the end of the relationship, they've not only lost a companion, but many of the intangibles that made them so special, and on top of that some of their money. I'm not saying that you won't spend money on the person you love but you don't have to become their bankroll, either! Love or what you think is love is blinding and over time, frivolous spending adds up. Be cautious with your spending! Guard your heart and mind, so you don't part with your precious dollars unnecessarily. I thought this man wanted me, but in truth, he only wanted what I could do for him. Because he allowed me to, I thought we were building something. We were building something, just not together. He took what I did for him to make himself look good for other women! He did this shamelessly and I was too glad to rid my life of him once he was finally exposed. I'm sure that you want to know how he even got this close to me. Well, when I met him, we had such a great interaction. I thought I was on to something with him. Over time, I got to know him better and decided to see what was there. I pursued with much more intentionality than he did but that's a revelation that took some time to realize. He said something to me that immediately endeared me to him and I've got to tell you, he was so right about me, but oh so wrong for me! After a year of wrangling with the decision about my look, he said to me, "Chanel, short hair is your superpower!" Those words meant the world to me! Over the next few years, we spent time pursuing a common interest, but I never felt as if our romantic connection was growing. I thought it would and even really thought that something should have happened, but it never materialized into a committed relationship. Be aware that if a person is not choosing you, nothing you do will change their mind. No gift, sexcapades, financial gift, or anything else will do it. If something does change, are you sure that you have what it takes to keep the connection strong once you remove the extra you're giving? Think about that for a moment. Your heart is good, and you want to find a person to love and love you in return. A love that also requires you to get real about who a person is or is not. Take a break, alter your schedule or pattern. Do something out of the norm that places the weight and responsibility of satisfying the relationship on them and see what you have. What's left if you remove your input? What do you have when you say no? What's left if you're not the one suggesting a date night or dinner? Some people don't have the capacity to love and receive true love and they aren't worth the effort! This is a truth that many of us haven't discovered until it's too late. Our heart is broken, sense of self-worth is shattered and worst of all, we have wasted time and resources on a person not worth a single measure of it. These people aren't always the villains we make them out to be. So many of them need deep healing and these failed relationships bring them face to face with a real time opportunity to consider their ways and the healing needed. Unfortunately, many won't confront their failures and instead just move on to another potentially damaging relationship.

As much as I wanted to blame him for his behavior, there was someone else at fault. Many times, our relationships suffer from secondhand trauma. In this instance, the trauma inflicted is rooted so far in past that the only output that the person knows is trauma. Subconsciously, every attempt at a healthy, loving relationship is distorted by actions that subvert healthy communication and expressions of love. If we invoke the theory of love languages, their love language is trauma and emotional sabotage. It's not enough to say they are in their own way; these problematic partners are a relational failure waiting to happen. They haven't been equipped with the tools to orchestrate nor participate in a healthy relationship, thus inflicting trauma on unsuspecting partners. In hindsight I can clearly see all the signs I missed in that relationship. It was one sided and drained my life of the energy to even consider another relationship. He constantly rejected me as a whole. If you don't want all of me, you don't want NONE of me! Once I decided to stop settling for the little that he had to give, I was done. He had hurt me and disrespected me for the last time! It's not really that he chose other women over me. Yes, other women... Repeatedly! He was only giving them the same measure of himself that he was leasing to me and our interactions. They gave him their bodies and he gave them a world full of problems... And to some of them a few babies. As mad as I could be about it, I'm sad these women are now tied to him forever. I do believe that anybody can change, but when you make inflicting trauma your identity, I will warn every soul that I can. While doing some self-reflection, I discovered that the areas in me that were magnetized by his traumatic output had to be healed for good. Trauma bonding requires two culpable people. Each of us were at fault and I was to blame for not rejecting his rejection. Did you know that was possible? Did you know that there's a healthy way to put a demand on your partner and relationship? If no one has ever told you, I will. When you have established healthy parameters for your relationship, be willing to abide by them and enforce them! There is nothing wrong with letting your partner know what you would like to see happen. Now don't be overbearing or think you can control the relationship but be clear in how you communicate what you desire. And if desires have been communicated to you, consider them and what they may mean to your partner. Also consider what not doing for them means. This is the space where trauma occurs. When our feelings and past experiences are not taken into serious consideration, we give our partners unhindered access to our deepest hurt and pain and most times, it's made worse. The compounding act of first accessing the past pain by inconsiderably disregarding us then inflicting new pain on top of it in the emotional/mental place where it happened is driving some of us crazy.

But you aren't crazy, you're traumatized! And how dare anyone put an expectation on any one of us to heal from a place they keep hurting us in. This is where so many relationships are. Because trauma is a love language and the way some people communicate love, I have to also confess that some people receive love through traumatic experiences. No, they're not asking their partner to traumatize them. There is a person in their past who had their heart but also traumatized them and when you do the same, they understand it as love on the same level as that person in their past. That's a headscratcher there, isn't it? Not exactly. Some people in this symbiotic situation have never parted. The glue holding their relationship together is trauma! It's not that one partner's heart is so big that they consistently accept cheating or have even "opened" the relationship or marriage, that acceptance is a bona fide trauma response. Have you ever tried to coax that afflicted spouse or partner to leave? It's no surprise that you are villainized and treated so poorly when you do. You're asking them to leave the person they love on levels they can't explain. As I mentioned earlier, their partner may do just enough to project feelings of love or relational security and they can't move on from it. This book challenges you to heal so that past trauma doesn't become present trauma. So many people in relationships are dysfunctional because relational trauma is at the root of their connection. You're asking a lot of two broken people in need of healing to find it, but it is possible. Be willing to do the work in your own life so that past trauma doesn't sink your relationship and be willing to fill your love tank so that partners don't drain and leave you empty. As you fill your love tank, put a demand on your partner, friends and family to give in return as much as they receive from you. That's not too much to ask, we've just spent too much time asking the wrong people and accepting too little in return. Be healed from trauma past and present and fill your love tank until it's overflowing!

This begins with a simple confession, "*I am fearfully and wonderfully made. I am worthy of love and I'm not at fault for the trauma inflicted on me. I rise from the ashes of brokenness, and I openly receive God's love and the love he gives me through my friends, family, and romantic partner. I am loved, I am whole, and I am healthy. I am who God says I am, and I will have what God says I can have.*"

THE COMMITMENT TO LOVE

I'S TIME TO say "I do" to you! Before I go any further talking about commitment, I need you to be willing to do the necessary work to be your best self. Before you're a better partner, spouse parent or friend, I need you to be the best you. Think about it, the world deserves the best possible version of you. This chapter will mention several commitments, but the main one is the one you make to yourself. Got it? Whatever work that's needed, commit to doing it. This may require a season of isolation and separation from romantic relationships, abstinence from sexual activity and the renewal of core values. For those of you in relationships whose work doesn't require a complete reset, commit to it and show up for your partner. Commit to being the person they need you to be, not merely the person you want to be. Healthy relationships endure the challenges of change that come with each phase in season! Don't be afraid to adapt, evolve and expand your capacity for relational knowledge. Expand your capacity for emotional intelligence and integrity. Commit to honesty and develop a sense of desire for your partner's well-being. I'm not asking you to put their well-being above yours any more than the Bible does, but I am asking for healthy consideration of your partner. This may be the part in your relationship when you realize that you're not meant for each other. You may also realize after reading this book that the bond you enjoy is destructive.

If that's the case, commit to a healthy end to the relationship that releases the both of you to the prospect of abundant love with other partners. The final commitment I want you to make is to the future of relationships in your life. Commit to putting your days of abuse, trauma, toxicity, betrayal, distrust and other peace robbing relationship dysfunction behind you! We are opening the door for abundant love and healthy relationships while slamming the door shut on all other instances of relational trauma. The highest level of commitment in relationships is marriage. A great friend shared with me that strong marriages are powered by a commitment to love. This commitment says I'm in this marriage regardless of what happens. Many of us come into marriages and relationships with a secret list and for some a not-so-secret list of deal breakers. Unknowingly, our unions are predisposed even if subconsciously falling to relational failure. We're prepared to pack it all in and leave when the unthinkable happens. What if your partner asked, "how deep is your love?" How would you answer that? Many of us can answer that with our list of deal breakers. Some of you could answer it with your hypotheticals. You already know that you wouldn't be willing to care for your partner if they were suddenly invalid. You wouldn't be willing to pick up the slack if your spouse's income went away. You may be certain that you don't have the bandwidth to support your partner through a mental episode but can that change? An overarching theme of this book is change. It's only an ugly word to people resistant to altering their life for the betterment of themselves and those that they are in relationship with. Change isn't ugly, it should be welcomed when you know the outcome is to the benefit of you and those you love. I'll share a story to help you embrace change when it impacts your interest.

As an athlete, injuries were common on the court. None of us were exempt from an ankle sprain, a jammed finger or jumper's knee. Injuries were inevitable, but we stayed on the court and in the game regardless of the known risk. I had a bout with an injury that was more annoying than hurtful. It required more stretching than icing and rest. Now, if I applied the methods of ice, heat, and rest, it would have gotten better over a longer period of time but as an athlete, movement is my way of life. How did I get over this injury? Stretching! I kid you not, when that ligament was stretched, I increased its pliability. The injury made the ligament rigid which was not its ideal condition. I treated the ligament and not a muscle. That's the other part of healing, healing in the right place.

Let's tell the truth here, some of us are willing to do everything besides what's necessary to heal and our relationships suffer because of it. We choose to put on ice and rest when we should be stretching! How pliable are you in your relationship? How pliable are your expectations, and even your deal breakers? Are you declaring "no deal" in scenarios that you could grant a "new deal?" Commitment requires you to become an agent of change unto yourself for the betterment of the relationship. Ask yourself, who or what is this relationship asking me to be or become. and am I willing to do it? Any unwillingness to stretch or be stretched nurtures the injury and not the intent of relationships. Commitment accepts the unknown future and says, "we can do it because I'm willing to do what's needed. I'm willing to evolve in my thinking and emotional output, I'm willing to be someone new for you!"

We are often afraid to change because in relationships it's seen as people losing themselves to their detriment, but in marriage, two become one! It's not instant and nothing about this change is automatic. This change puts a demand on past relationships, past trauma, learned behaviors, and anything else that can be changed. It's no mistake that the need for change shows up in our relationships as the sign of a new season on the horizon! So, commit to doing the work of evolving when called upon. Our greatest hope in love and relationships is that we have someone willing to evolve with us. We need them to be our resting place when our world shifts into new seasons. We need them to be patient with us as our bodies and do a physical and even mental changes. Choose wisely though! Some changes are so tumultuous that it threatens the strength of the bond you share.,. Despite this threat, a committed partner is ready with a life preserver and even willing to get in the lifeboat with you should you find yourself shipwrecked as the billows that wreck partnerships roll. Real partnership is a matter of relationship!

EPILOGUE

I F YOU ARE intentional about making your relationships and friend-ships work, you must gain an understanding of their feelings. Take time to learn how they feel when there is a conflict or in moments too difficult for words. We all respond to life differently and our emotional intelligence is just as varied as all other compo-nents of a relationship. To better help maneuver through the hard work and challenges that come with doing the relational work in this book, I'm sharing the feelings wheel with you. I use the feeling wheel to see what I want to say in emotionally charged moments. By learning the corresponding feelings and emotions, I'm able to refer to them and recall them with better command. This feeling wheel also shows the extensions and layers of our emotional out-put. Many times, naming the surface emotion doesn't suffice and the superficial nature of our understanding only adds to the prob-lem. Are you hurt or are you disappointed? That breakup made you bitter, but why? Would you agree that you're bitter about it? Adding specificity to the conversations allows us to also pave the way for transparency in our lives and relationships. By owning your feelings and seeing which feelings are gateways to others, you allow yourself a chance to amend the behaviors necessary to expe-rience a complete behavioral change. The feelings will also present an opportunity for redirection. As you learn which feelings are common responses, seek out better, positive feelings which will lead to better responses. My go to feeling is "I'm frustrated," but this is an incomplete answer. Behind "frustrated" is, hurt, anxious, insecure, disappointed, and powerlessness. I use "frustrated" as a general response to negativity. This way, I can avoid vulnerability because no one wants to deal with a woman when she's frustrated!

I'm learning to open the door to resolution and reconciliation though. If I'm hurt and not just frustrated, I'm learning to express that in a healthy way because I can actually see the wheel turning that negative to a positive. Relationships matter, but relationship issues like forgiveness, establishing boundaries, communication, compromise, and healing all require that we're in touch with our feelings and emotions. Knowing which feelings to present in certain situations give us an opportunity to self-reflect and redirect. Yes, you're going to want to disengage those triggers! Going off and being explosive as a regular response shorten the shelf life of your relationships and friendships and is the antithesis of this book's aim! Don't be afraid of change, even if the only change you experience is identifying your feelings. You can't be afraid of baby steps because they indicate that you want to get moving on your own volition and that deserves recognition and praise on your behalf. Congratulations on your new journey to emotional health and Wellness. May the future of your relationships and friendships be as bright as the sun in the summertime! I want to hear from you! Bring me along on your journey, I'll be waiting to hear from you on all my social channels. Stay tuned because we'll be discussing many of these topics in the book on upcoming CheMinistry shows. Consider yourself invited because I can't wait to see you there!

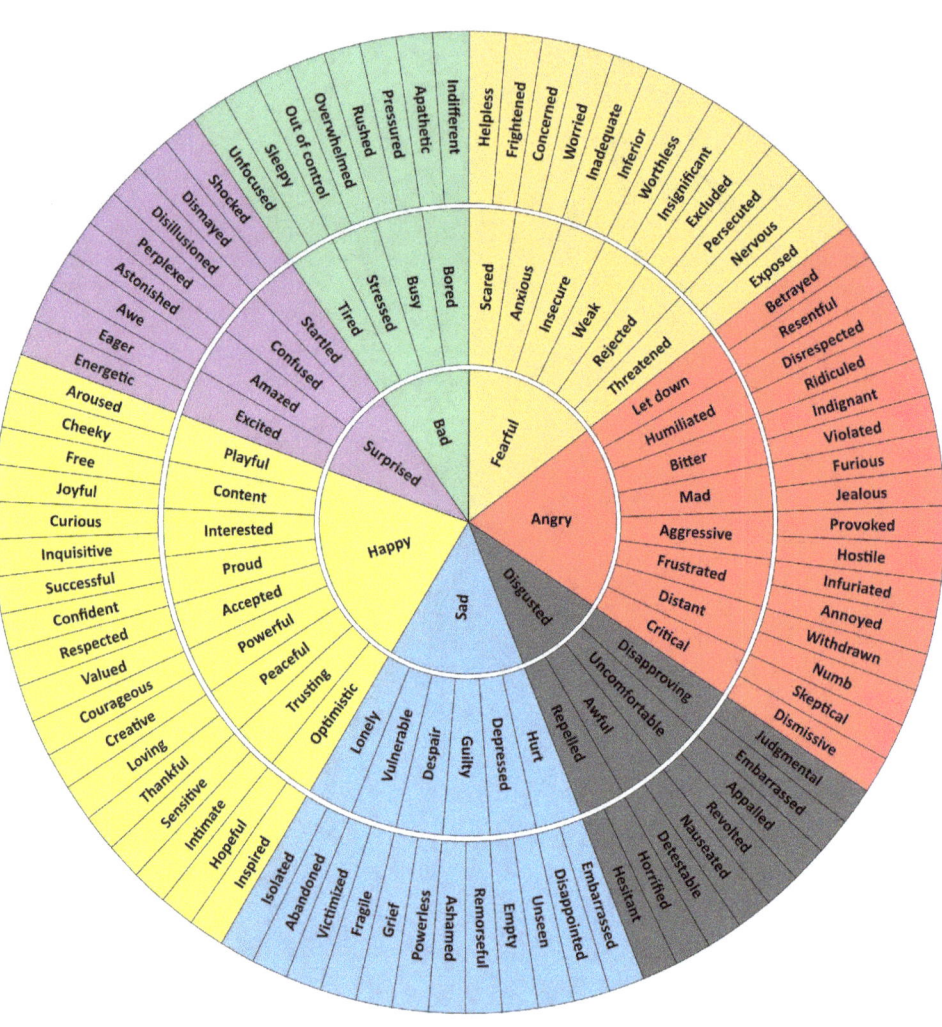

THE FEELINGS WHEEL

USED BY PERMISSION of Geoffrey Roberts (Whitehouse Church in Australia), the Feelings Wheel will help you better articulate what you feel in a way that is easily understood by you and the people in your life. Use this apparatus to examine your life and your resonance to life's events. Start by assessing your feelings after reading "Relationships Matter." How has the book made you feel? How do you feel about the information in the book?

As an extended exercise, try assessing how you feel about your current romantic relationship. Are there any other relationships (friendships, family, co-worker) that you would like to assess? Feel free to use the wheel. Speaking the truth about our relationships will give us clarity about the way they make us feel and better inform our ensuing actions. You may even discover that you need to make improvements and alterations to what you're doing. Remember, this book has given you the tools to communicate your feelings in a more productive way that not only nurtures but deepens the romantic connection shared by those who are intentional about growing their romantic relationship.

RELATIONSHIPS MATTER
(REFLECTIONS ON THE BOOK)

IN THIS SECTION, I want you to reflect on this book. This is your chance to be candid and write your thoughts about the questions posed from select chapters. "Relationships Matter" was written to help readers grow through many of the challenges that plague relationships and keep us from becoming our best selves. Your answers will help you commit to reaching your highest ideals and help improve the quality of your relationship by introducing vulnerability, transparency and truth into the way you see yourself and your partner.

DOING THE WORK

What does "doing the work" mean to you?

_____

_____

_____

_____

_____

_____

_____

_____

YOU NEED THIS, NOT THAT!

Have you discovered your life's purpose?

_____

_____

_____

_____

_____

_____

_____

_____

EXTRACTING YOUR EMOTIONS

How do your emotions inform your decisions within your relationships?

_____

_____

_____

_____

_____

_____

_____

_____

How do you establish emotional integrity in your relationships?

Describe your process of learning your partner's emotional strengths and weaknesses.

_____

_____

_____

_____

_____

_____

_____

_____

How do you ward off emotional sabotage in your relationships?

_____

_____

_____

_____

_____

_____

_____

_____

GIVE THE GIFT OF FORGIVENESS

Is it easy for you to forgive others?

_____

_____

_____

_____

_____

_____

_____

_____

Do you struggle with forgiving yourself?

_____

_____

_____

_____

_____

_____

_____

_____

Can a person truly forgive and forget?

Are you holding on to any hurt that you need to let go of?

_____

_____

_____

_____

_____

_____

_____

_____

ESTABLISHING HEALTHY BOUNDARIES

How do you set healthy boundaries?

What are your boundaries in a relationship?

_____

_____

_____

_____

_____

_____

_____

_____

Do boundaries vary in your romantic or platonic relationships?

_____

_____

_____

_____

_____

_____

_____

_____

What is your response to a violation of your boundaries?

_____

_____

_____

_____

_____

_____

_____

_____

Forgivable or deal breaker, your thoughts on boundary violations?

WHAT IT MEANS TO ME

Define the mutual respect you expect in your relationship?

**Would you apologize if your partner
told you that something you said
or did was disrespectful?**

_____

_____

_____

_____

_____

_____

_____

_____

DO YOU HEAR YOURSELF?

Do you ever check to ensure that your actions match your words?

_____

_____

_____

_____

_____

_____

_____

_____

Have you ever been gaslit when trying to hold your partner accountable for what they've said?

_____

_____

_____

_____

_____

_____

_____

_____

YOU'RE NOT CRAZY, YOU'RE TRAUMATIZED!

What steps did you take to heal from past relational trauma?

_____

_____

_____

_____

_____

_____

_____

_____

How has trauma from the past affected your relationship?

THE COMMITMENT TO LOVE

How Strong Is Your Commitment
to a Healthy Relationship?

Have You Identified Any Possible Barriers to a Healthy Relationship?

_____

_____

_____

_____

_____

_____

_____

_____

BIBLIOGRAPHY

Merriam-Webster. (n.d.). *Lust definition & meaning*. Merriam Webster. Retrieved March 10, 2022, from https://www. merriam-webster.com/dictionary/lust

Merriam-Webster. (n.d.). *Forgiveness definition & meaning*. Merriam-Webster. Retrieved May 3, 2022, from https://www. merriam-webster.com/dictionary/lust

Emotion. emotion noun - Definition, pictures, pronunciation and usage notes | Oxford Advanced Learner's Dictionary at xfordLearnersDictionaries.com. (n.d.). Retrieved June 10, 2022, from https://www.oxfordlearnersdictionaries.com/us/ definition/english/emotion?q=emotions

Merriam-Webster. (n.d.). *Trauma definition & meaning*. Merriam Webster. Retrieved January 21, 2022, from https://www. merriam-webster.com/dictionary/lust

CHANEL N. SCOTT

CHANEL N. SCOTT is a prominent figure in the romantic relational sphere who in 2015 created CheMinistry, a relationship platform. Today, CheMinistry is a television series on Fox Soul that consists of conversations about romance and relationships moderated by Chanel. Each panel discussion features celebrities and influencers who share experiential knowledge and expertise pertaining to thematic conversations about romantic relationships. Notably, the "Queen of Relationship Talk," Chanel evokes transparent and candid dialogue on relational topics specifically geared toward sustaining intimate relationships between a man and a woman.

Chanel jump-starts the conversation by exploring the varying nuances of 21st-century romantic relationships. By first peeling back the layers of some of the more critical issues plaguing romantic relationships in today's culture, the conversation creates a safety zone for panelists to acknowledge their fears, insecurities, and pain to help create a keener sense of awareness and a more objective perspective. Chanel strongly believes that acknowledging our fears, insecurities, and pain will help create a new sense of awareness and a more objective perspective as the conversation ensues.

In order to appreciate CheMinistry, you must understand the woman behind it, how she views the world, the struggles she's faced, and the enormous giants she fought through to get herself and the brand (one and the same) to where it is today. In her reign as the Queen of Relationship Talk, Chanel makes the stage a safe space and sounding board for panelists to communicate vulnerabilities while discussing intimate, complex relationship issues. You see, CheMinistry is not just another artistic and innovative idea. It's a philosophy, state of mind, and collage of experiences that emerged from Chanel's life. It rivets the mind and the senses. CheMinistry is the embodiment of an interwoven process that tells Chanel's story and flows to its next relationship platform.

WHAT IS CheMinistry?

TO SOME, CURIOSITY is a killer, but to Chanel N. Scott, it was an inspiration. After several years of unfruitful relationships, Chanel grew curious about the chronic missteps that doomed her romantic relationships. While she knew there was much intrapersonal work needed, she sought to create a safe space for men to share their perspectives without condemnation. With that, CheMinistry was born.

CheMinistry joined the FOX SOUL family in May 2022 and became the newest member of their community of creatives. Chanel has seen her vision manifested right before her eyes and considers it to be the opportunity of a lifetime. CheMinistry values are articulated through FOX SOUL's vision to inspire, inform, educate, and entertain viewers.

CheMinistry is a relationship platform created to bridge the gap between purpose-driven men and women who desire to progressively move their love life to the next level. We've all experienced the disappointment of watching enthrallment dissipate as without warning, the chemistry of our relationship changes. Suddenly, the calls cease, the texts disappear and before you know it, your budding romance has reached stagnation.

There is nothing that requires more courage than sustaining an intimate relationship. Vulnerability is incredibly difficult to achieve and even more difficult to share. Revealing your deepest fears and insecurities to another person can be frightening and even discourage you from pursuing healthy relationships. It's no surprise that so many people choose to forego vulnerability and relationships altogether, opting instead to live their lives on the surface, never forming a lasting connection with another person. We want to give you the tools to achieve and receive abundant love. You can abound in love and as a lover, but it is not an accident.

www.ingramcontent.com/pod-product-compliance
Lightning Source LLC
Chambersburg PA
CBHW071405120626
46546CB00002B/814